C000003922

Sales Leader
Complete Self-Assessment Guide

The guidance in this Self-Assessment is based on Sales Leader best practices and standards in business process architecture, design and quality management. The guidance is also based on the professional judgment of the individual collaborators listed in the Acknowledgments.

Notice of rights

You are licensed to use the Self-Assessment contents in your presentations and materials for internal use and customers without asking us - we are here to help.

Trademarks

Many of the designations used by manufacturers and sellers to distinguish their products are claimed as trademarks. Where those designations appear in this book, and the publisher was aware of a trademark claim, the designations appear as requested by the owner of the trademark. All other product names and services identified throughout this book are used in editorial fashion only and for the benefit of such companies with no intention of infringement of the trademark. No such use, or the use of any trade name, is intended to convey endorsement or other affiliation with this book.

Copyright © by The Art of Service
http://theartofservice.com
service@theartofservice.com

Table of Contents

About The Art of Service 7

Acknowledgments 8

Included Resources - how to access 9

Your feedback is invaluable to us 11

Purpose of this Self-Assessment 11

How to use the Self-Assessment 12

Sales Leader

Scorecard Example 14

Sales Leader

Scorecard 15

BEGINNING OF THE

SELF-ASSESSMENT: 16

CRITERION #1: RECOGNIZE 17

CRITERION #2: DEFINE: 28

CRITERION #3: MEASURE: 43

CRITERION #4: ANALYZE: 58

CRITERION #5: IMPROVE: 74

CRITERION #6: CONTROL: 89

CRITERION #7: SUSTAIN: 101

Sales Leader and Managing Projects, Criteria for Project

Managers: 126

1.0 Initiating Process Group: Sales Leader 127

1.1 Project Charter: Sales Leader 129

1.2 Stakeholder Register: Sales Leader 131

1.3 Stakeholder Analysis Matrix: Sales Leader 132

2.0 Planning Process Group: Sales Leader 134

2.1 Project Management Plan: Sales Leader 136

2.2 Scope Management Plan: Sales Leader 138

2.3 Requirements Management Plan: Sales Leader 140

2.4 Requirements Documentation: Sales Leader 142

2.5 Requirements Traceability Matrix: Sales Leader 144

2.6 Project Scope Statement: Sales Leader 146

2.7 Assumption and Constraint Log: Sales Leader 148

2.8 Work Breakdown Structure: Sales Leader 150

2.9 WBS Dictionary: Sales Leader 152

2.10 Schedule Management Plan: Sales Leader 154

2.11 Activity List: Sales Leader 156

2.12 Activity Attributes: Sales Leader 158

2.13 Milestone List: Sales Leader 160

2.14 Network Diagram: Sales Leader 162

2.15 Activity Resource Requirements: Sales Leader 164

2.16 Resource Breakdown Structure: Sales Leader 166

2.17 Activity Duration Estimates: Sales Leader 168

2.18 Duration Estimating Worksheet: Sales Leader 170

2.19 Project Schedule: Sales Leader 172

2.20 Cost Management Plan: Sales Leader 174

2.21 Activity Cost Estimates: Sales Leader 176

2.22 Cost Estimating Worksheet: Sales Leader 178

2.23 Cost Baseline: Sales Leader 180

2.24 Quality Management Plan: Sales Leader 182

2.25 Quality Metrics: Sales Leader 184

2.26 Process Improvement Plan: Sales Leader 186

2.27 Responsibility Assignment Matrix: Sales Leader 188

2.28 Roles and Responsibilities: Sales Leader 190

2.29 Human Resource Management Plan: Sales Leader 192

2.30 Communications Management Plan: Sales Leader 194

2.31 Risk Management Plan: Sales Leader 196

2.32 Risk Register: Sales Leader 198

2.33 Probability and Impact Assessment: Sales Leader 200

2.34 Probability and Impact Matrix: Sales Leader 202

2.35 Risk Data Sheet: Sales Leader 204

2.36 Procurement Management Plan: Sales Leader 206

2.37 Source Selection Criteria: Sales Leader   208

2.38 Stakeholder Management Plan: Sales Leader   210

2.39 Change Management Plan: Sales Leader   212

3.0 Executing Process Group: Sales Leader   214

3.1 Team Member Status Report: Sales Leader   216

3.2 Change Request: Sales Leader   218

3.3 Change Log: Sales Leader   220

3.4 Decision Log: Sales Leader   222

3.5 Quality Audit: Sales Leader   224

3.6 Team Directory: Sales Leader   227

3.7 Team Operating Agreement: Sales Leader   229

3.8 Team Performance Assessment: Sales Leader   231

3.9 Team Member Performance Assessment: Sales Leader   233

3.10 Issue Log: Sales Leader   235

4.0 Monitoring and Controlling Process Group: Sales Leader   237

4.1 Project Performance Report: Sales Leader   239

4.2 Variance Analysis: Sales Leader   241

4.3 Earned Value Status: Sales Leader   243

4.4 Risk Audit: Sales Leader   245

4.5 Contractor Status Report: Sales Leader   247

4.6 Formal Acceptance: Sales Leader   249

5.0 Closing Process Group: Sales Leader   251

5.1 Procurement Audit: Sales Leader   253

5.2 Contract Close-Out: Sales Leader   255

5.3 Project or Phase Close-Out: Sales Leader   257

5.4 Lessons Learned: Sales Leader   259
Index   261

About The Art of Service

The Art of Service, Business Process Architects since 2000, is dedicated to helping stakeholders achieve excellence.

Defining, designing, creating, and implementing a process to solve a stakeholders challenge or meet an objective is the most valuable role... In EVERY group, company, organization and department.

Unless you're talking a one-time, single-use project, there should be a process. Whether that process is managed and implemented by humans, AI, or a combination of the two, it needs to be designed by someone with a complex enough perspective to ask the right questions.

Someone capable of asking the right questions and step back and say, 'What are we really trying to accomplish here? And is there a different way to look at it?'

With The Art of Service's Standard Requirements Self-Assessments, we empower people who can do just that — whether their title is marketer, entrepreneur, manager, salesperson, consultant, Business Process Manager, executive assistant, IT Manager, CIO etc... —they are the people who rule the future. They are people who watch the process as it happens, and ask the right questions to make the process work better.

Contact us when you need any support with this Self-Assessment and any help with templates, blue-prints and examples of standard documents you might need:

http://theartofservice.com
service@theartofservice.com

Acknowledgments

This checklist was developed under the auspices of The Art of Service, chaired by Gerardus Blokdyk.

Representatives from several client companies participated in the preparation of this Self-Assessment.

In addition, we are thankful for the design and printing services provided.

Included Resources - how to access

Included with your purchase of the book is the Sales Leader Self-Assessment Spreadsheet Dashboard which contains all questions and Self-Assessment areas and auto-generates insights, graphs, and project RACI planning - all with examples to get you started right away.

How? Simply send an email to
access@theartofservice.com
with this books' title in the subject to get the Sales Leader Self Assessment Tool right away.

You will receive the following contents with New and Updated specific criteria:

- The latest quick edition of the book in PDF

- The latest complete edition of the book in PDF, which criteria correspond to the criteria in...

- The Self-Assessment Excel Dashboard, and...

- Example pre-filled Self-Assessment Excel Dashboard to get familiar with results generation

- In-depth specific Checklists covering the topic

- Project management checklists and templates to assist with implementation

INCLUDES LIFETIME SELF ASSESSMENT UPDATES

Every self assessment comes with Lifetime Updates and Lifetime Free Updated Books. Lifetime Updates is an industry-first feature which allows you to receive verified self assessment updates, ensuring you always have the most accurate information at your fingertips.

Get it now- you will be glad you did - do it now, before you forget.

Send an email to **access@theartofservice.com** with this books' title in the subject to get the Sales Leader Self Assessment Tool right away.

Your feedback is invaluable to us

If you recently bought this book, we would love to hear from you! You can do this by writing a review on amazon (or the online store where you purchased this book) about your last purchase! As part of our continual service improvement process, we love to hear real client experiences and feedback.

How does it work?
To post a review on Amazon, just log in to your account and click on the Create Your Own Review button (under Customer Reviews) of the relevant product page. You can find examples of product reviews in Amazon. If you purchased from another online store, simply follow their procedures.

What happens when I submit my review?
Once you have submitted your review, send us an email at review@theartofservice.com with the link to your review so we can properly thank you for your feedback.

Purpose of this Self-Assessment

This Self-Assessment has been developed to improve understanding of the requirements and elements of Sales Leader, based on best practices and standards in business process architecture, design and quality management.

It is designed to allow for a rapid Self-Assessment to determine how closely existing management practices and procedures correspond to the elements of the Self-Assessment.

The criteria of requirements and elements of Sales Leader have been rephrased in the format of a Self-Assessment questionnaire, with a seven-criterion scoring system, as explained in this document.

In this format, even with limited background knowledge of

Sales Leader, a manager can quickly review existing operations to determine how they measure up to the standards. This in turn can serve as the starting point of a 'gap analysis' to identify management tools or system elements that might usefully be implemented in the organization to help improve overall performance.

How to use the Self-Assessment

On the following pages are a series of questions to identify to what extent your Sales Leader initiative is complete in comparison to the requirements set in standards.

To facilitate answering the questions, there is a space in front of each question to enter a score on a scale of '1' to '5'.

1 Strongly Disagree

2 Disagree

3 Neutral

4 Agree

5 Strongly Agree

Read the question and rate it with the following in front of mind:

'In my belief,
the answer to this question is clearly defined'.

There are two ways in which you can choose to interpret this statement;
1. how aware are you that the answer to the question is clearly defined
2. for more in-depth analysis you can choose to gather

evidence and confirm the answer to the question. This obviously will take more time, most Self-Assessment users opt for the first way to interpret the question and dig deeper later on based on the outcome of the overall Self-Assessment.

A score of '1' would mean that the answer is not clear at all, where a '5' would mean the answer is crystal clear and defined. Leave emtpy when the question is not applicable or you don't want to answer it, you can skip it without affecting your score. Write your score in the space provided.

After you have responded to all the appropriate statements in each section, compute your average score for that section, using the formula provided, and round to the nearest tenth. Then transfer to the corresponding spoke in the Sales Leader Scorecard on the second next page of the Self-Assessment.

Your completed Sales Leader Scorecard will give you a clear presentation of which Sales Leader areas need attention.

Sales Leader
Scorecard Example

Example of how the finalized Scorecard can look like:

Sales Leader Scorecard

Your Scores:

BEGINNING OF THE
SELF-ASSESSMENT:

CRITERION #1: RECOGNIZE

INTENT: Be aware of the need for change. Recognize that there is an unfavorable variation, problem or symptom.

In my belief, the answer to this question is clearly defined:

5 Strongly Agree

4 Agree

3 Neutral

2 Disagree

1 Strongly Disagree

1. Does Sales Leader create potential expectations in other areas that need to be recognized and considered?
<--- Score

2. Does the problem have ethical dimensions?
<--- Score

3. What Sales Leader problem should be solved?

<--- Score

4. To what extent would your organization benefit from being recognized as a award recipient?
<--- Score

5. Are employees recognized for desired behaviors?
<--- Score

6. How do you identify the kinds of information that you will need?
<--- Score

7. Who defines the rules in relation to any given issue?
<--- Score

8. What activities does the governance board need to consider?
<--- Score

9. How do you assess your Sales Leader workforce capability and capacity needs, including skills, competencies, and staffing levels?
<--- Score

10. What do you need to start doing?
<--- Score

11. What are the Sales Leader resources needed?
<--- Score

12. Will Sales Leader deliverables need to be tested and, if so, by whom?
<--- Score

13. What are the expected benefits of Sales Leader to

the stakeholder?
<--- Score

14. Is it needed?
<--- Score

15. What extra resources will you need?
<--- Score

16. Are there Sales Leader problems defined?
<--- Score

17. What Sales Leader capabilities do you need?
<--- Score

18. What are the stakeholder objectives to be achieved with Sales Leader?
<--- Score

19. Is the need for organizational change recognized?
<--- Score

20. What creative shifts do you need to take?
<--- Score

21. What Sales Leader coordination do you need?
<--- Score

22. What situation(s) led to this Sales Leader Self Assessment?
<--- Score

23. Which needs are not included or involved?
<--- Score

24. What is the smallest subset of the problem you

can usefully solve?

<--- Score

25. Who needs budgets?

<--- Score

26. What should be considered when identifying available resources, constraints, and deadlines?

<--- Score

27. Do you need to avoid or amend any Sales Leader activities?

<--- Score

28. Do you know what you need to know about Sales Leader?

<--- Score

29. What vendors make products that address the Sales Leader needs?

<--- Score

30. How are training requirements identified?

<--- Score

31. Which issues are too important to ignore?

<--- Score

32. What are your needs in relation to Sales Leader skills, labor, equipment, and markets?

<--- Score

33. Will a response program recognize when a crisis occurs and provide some level of response?

<--- Score

34. What would happen if Sales Leader weren't done?
<--- Score

35. What is the extent or complexity of the Sales Leader problem?
<--- Score

36. What are the minority interests and what amount of minority interests can be recognized?
<--- Score

37. Whom do you really need or want to serve?
<--- Score

38. What is the recognized need?
<--- Score

39. What training and capacity building actions are needed to implement proposed reforms?
<--- Score

40. How much are sponsors, customers, partners, stakeholders involved in Sales Leader? In other words, what are the risks, if Sales Leader does not deliver successfully?
<--- Score

41. Who else hopes to benefit from it?
<--- Score

42. Can management personnel recognize the monetary benefit of Sales Leader?
<--- Score

43. Is the quality assurance team identified?
<--- Score

44. Are controls defined to recognize and contain problems?
<--- Score

45. What needs to stay?
<--- Score

46. Are you dealing with any of the same issues today as yesterday? What can you do about this?
<--- Score

47. Who needs what information?
<--- Score

48. As a sponsor, customer or management, how important is it to meet goals, objectives?
<--- Score

49. How are the Sales Leader's objectives aligned to the group's overall stakeholder strategy?
<--- Score

50. What problems are you facing and how do you consider Sales Leader will circumvent those obstacles?
<--- Score

51. What else needs to be measured?
<--- Score

52. Where do you need to exercise leadership?
<--- Score

53. Who should resolve the Sales Leader issues?
<--- Score

54. Does your organization need more Sales Leader education?
<--- Score

55. Why the need?
<--- Score

56. What Sales Leader events should you attend?
<--- Score

57. Are employees recognized or rewarded for performance that demonstrates the highest levels of integrity?
<--- Score

58. Which information does the Sales Leader business case need to include?
<--- Score

59. What resources or support might you need?
<--- Score

60. What does Sales Leader success mean to the stakeholders?
<--- Score

61. Do you have/need 24-hour access to key personnel?
<--- Score

62. Consider your own Sales Leader project, what types of organizational problems do you think might be causing or affecting your problem, based on the work done so far?
<--- Score

63. What is the problem or issue?
<--- Score

64. What are the timeframes required to resolve each of the issues/problems?
<--- Score

65. Think about the people you identified for your Sales Leader project and the project responsibilities you would assign to them, what kind of training do you think they would need to perform these responsibilities effectively?
<--- Score

66. Who needs to know?
<--- Score

67. Looking at each person individually – does every one have the qualities which are needed to work in this group?
<--- Score

68. What prevents you from making the changes you know will make you a more effective Sales Leader leader?
<--- Score

69. Who needs to know about Sales Leader?
<--- Score

70. How are you going to measure success?
<--- Score

71. Do you recognize Sales Leader achievements?
<--- Score

72. Are your goals realistic? Do you need to redefine your problem? Perhaps the problem has changed or maybe you have reached your goal and need to set a new one?
<--- Score

73. For your Sales Leader project, identify and describe the business environment, is there more than one layer to the business environment?
<--- Score

74. How do you recognize an objection?
<--- Score

75. What do employees need in the short term?
<--- Score

76. Where is training needed?
<--- Score

77. What information do users need?
<--- Score

78. What are the clients issues and concerns?
<--- Score

79. Are losses recognized in a timely manner?
<--- Score

80. What is the problem and/or vulnerability?
<--- Score

81. Would you recognize a threat from the inside?
<--- Score

82. Is it clear when you think of the day ahead of you

what activities and tasks you need to complete?
<--- Score

83. Are there any revenue recognition issues?
<--- Score

84. How can auditing be a preventative security measure?
<--- Score

85. How many trainings, in total, are needed?
<--- Score

86. Why is this needed?
<--- Score

87. When a Sales Leader manager recognizes a problem, what options are available?
<--- Score

88. Will it solve real problems?
<--- Score

89. What needs to be done?
<--- Score

90. Are problem definition and motivation clearly presented?
<--- Score

91. How does it fit into your organizational needs and tasks?
<--- Score

92. Are there any specific expectations or concerns about the Sales Leader team, Sales Leader itself?

<--- Score

93. Are there recognized Sales Leader problems?
<--- Score

94. Did you miss any major Sales Leader issues?
<--- Score

95. What tools and technologies are needed for a custom Sales Leader project?
<--- Score

Add up total points for this section:
_____ = Total points for this section

Divided by: _____ (number of statements answered) = _____
Average score for this section

Transfer your score to the Sales Leader Index at the beginning of the Self-Assessment.

CRITERION #2: DEFINE:

INTENT: Formulate the stakeholder problem. Define the problem, needs and objectives.

In my belief, the answer to this question is clearly defined:

5 Strongly Agree

4 Agree

3 Neutral

2 Disagree

1 Strongly Disagree

1. Has a team charter been developed and communicated?
<--- Score

2. Do the problem and goal statements meet the SMART criteria (specific, measurable, attainable, relevant, and time-bound)?
<--- Score

3. In what way can you redefine the criteria of choice clients have in your category in your favor?
<--- Score

4. Has/have the customer(s) been identified?
<--- Score

5. What defines best in class?
<--- Score

6. Are different versions of process maps needed to account for the different types of inputs?
<--- Score

7. How have you defined all Sales Leader requirements first?
<--- Score

8. What are the requirements for audit information?
<--- Score

9. What sources do you use to gather information for a Sales Leader study?
<--- Score

10. Are there any constraints known that bear on the ability to perform Sales Leader work? How is the team addressing them?
<--- Score

11. Is Sales Leader linked to key stakeholder goals and objectives?
<--- Score

12. Does the team have regular meetings?
<--- Score

13. Is there regularly 100% attendance at the team meetings? If not, have appointed substitutes attended to preserve cross-functionality and full representation?
<--- Score

14. What Sales Leader requirements should be gathered?
<--- Score

15. Who is gathering Sales Leader information?
<--- Score

16. The political context: who holds power?
<--- Score

17. How do you catch Sales Leader definition inconsistencies?
<--- Score

18. Is there a clear Sales Leader case definition?
<--- Score

19. Scope of sensitive information?
<--- Score

20. How do you manage unclear Sales Leader requirements?
<--- Score

21. Have all basic functions of Sales Leader been defined?
<--- Score

22. Has your scope been defined?

<--- Score

23. How was the 'as is' process map developed, reviewed, verified and validated?
<--- Score

24. What are the compelling stakeholder reasons for embarking on Sales Leader?
<--- Score

25. Has the improvement team collected the 'voice of the customer' (obtained feedback – qualitative and quantitative)?
<--- Score

26. What is in scope?
<--- Score

27. When is the estimated completion date?
<--- Score

28. Do you all define Sales Leader in the same way?
<--- Score

29. What system do you use for gathering Sales Leader information?
<--- Score

30. Do you have a Sales Leader success story or case study ready to tell and share?
<--- Score

31. How do you build the right business case?
<--- Score

32. What intelligence can you gather?

<--- Score

33. Has a project plan, Gantt chart, or similar been developed/completed?
<--- Score

34. What are the record-keeping requirements of Sales Leader activities?
<--- Score

35. What Sales Leader services do you require?
<--- Score

36. What specifically is the problem? Where does it occur? When does it occur? What is its extent?
<--- Score

37. Is the team adequately staffed with the desired cross-functionality? If not, what additional resources are available to the team?
<--- Score

38. Is the work to date meeting requirements?
<--- Score

39. What is the scope of the Sales Leader work?
<--- Score

40. How does the Sales Leader manager ensure against scope creep?
<--- Score

41. Is special Sales Leader user knowledge required?
<--- Score

42. Are approval levels defined for contracts and

supplements to contracts?
<--- Score

43. What are the rough order estimates on cost savings/opportunities that Sales Leader brings?
<--- Score

44. Is it clearly defined in and to your organization what you do?
<--- Score

45. How will the Sales Leader team and the group measure complete success of Sales Leader?
<--- Score

46. What is out-of-scope initially?
<--- Score

47. Have the customer needs been translated into specific, measurable requirements? How?
<--- Score

48. What happens if Sales Leader's scope changes?
<--- Score

49. Is Sales Leader currently on schedule according to the plan?
<--- Score

50. Are the Sales Leader requirements complete?
<--- Score

51. What are the tasks and definitions?
<--- Score

52. Are audit criteria, scope, frequency and methods

defined?
<--- Score

53. What gets examined?
<--- Score

54. What is in the scope and what is not in scope?
<--- Score

55. Are the Sales Leader requirements testable?
<--- Score

56. What customer feedback methods were used to solicit their input?
<--- Score

57. Is the Sales Leader scope manageable?
<--- Score

58. How are consistent Sales Leader definitions important?
<--- Score

59. Is the improvement team aware of the different versions of a process: what they think it is vs. what it actually is vs. what it should be vs. what it could be?
<--- Score

60. What critical content must be communicated – who, what, when, where, and how?
<--- Score

61. What is out of scope?
<--- Score

62. What is a worst-case scenario for losses?

<--- Score

63. What are the Sales Leader tasks and definitions?
<--- Score

64. Will a Sales Leader production readiness review be required?
<--- Score

65. What would be the goal or target for a Sales Leader's improvement team?
<--- Score

66. Is there a critical path to deliver Sales Leader results?
<--- Score

67. What baselines are required to be defined and managed?
<--- Score

68. How do you gather Sales Leader requirements?
<--- Score

69. Has the direction changed at all during the course of Sales Leader? If so, when did it change and why?
<--- Score

70. How do you think the partners involved in Sales Leader would have defined success?
<--- Score

71. How do you keep key subject matter experts in the loop?
<--- Score

72. What sort of initial information to gather?
<--- Score

73. How often are the team meetings?
<--- Score

74. Has a high-level 'as is' process map been completed, verified and validated?
<--- Score

75. How do you hand over Sales Leader context?
<--- Score

76. Are all requirements met?
<--- Score

77. Have specific policy objectives been defined?
<--- Score

78. How do you gather requirements?
<--- Score

79. Who approved the Sales Leader scope?
<--- Score

80. Are resources adequate for the scope?
<--- Score

81. What is the definition of Sales Leader excellence?
<--- Score

82. Is the scope of Sales Leader defined?
<--- Score

83. What scope to assess?
<--- Score

84. What knowledge or experience is required?
<--- Score

85. What is the scope?
<--- Score

86. What information do you gather?
<--- Score

87. Has everyone on the team, including the team leaders, been properly trained?
<--- Score

88. How do you gather the stories?
<--- Score

89. What is the definition of success?
<--- Score

90. What are the dynamics of the communication plan?
<--- Score

91. What constraints exist that might impact the team?
<--- Score

92. What are the boundaries of the scope? What is in bounds and what is not? What is the start point? What is the stop point?
<--- Score

93. When is/was the Sales Leader start date?
<--- Score

94. Do you have organizational privacy requirements?
<--- Score

95. What scope do you want your strategy to cover?
<--- Score

96. Are accountability and ownership for Sales Leader clearly defined?
<--- Score

97. When are meeting minutes sent out? Who is on the distribution list?
<--- Score

98. How and when will the baselines be defined?
<--- Score

99. What was the context?
<--- Score

100. Is the current 'as is' process being followed? If not, what are the discrepancies?
<--- Score

101. How do you manage changes in Sales Leader requirements?
<--- Score

102. If substitutes have been appointed, have they been briefed on the Sales Leader goals and received regular communications as to the progress to date?
<--- Score

103. What is the scope of the Sales Leader effort?
<--- Score

104. How did the Sales Leader manager receive input to the development of a Sales Leader improvement plan and the estimated completion dates/times of each activity?
<--- Score

105. What is the scope of Sales Leader?
<--- Score

106. Are task requirements clearly defined?
<--- Score

107. How will variation in the actual durations of each activity be dealt with to ensure that the expected Sales Leader results are met?
<--- Score

108. What information should you gather?
<--- Score

109. Is the Sales Leader scope complete and appropriately sized?
<--- Score

110. Is Sales Leader required?
<--- Score

111. Has a Sales Leader requirement not been met?
<--- Score

112. How would you define the culture at your organization, how susceptible is it to Sales Leader changes?
<--- Score

113. Is scope creep really all bad news?

<--- Score

114. Are required metrics defined, what are they?
<--- Score

115. Why are you doing Sales Leader and what is the scope?
<--- Score

116. What are the Roles and Responsibilities for each team member and its leadership? Where is this documented?
<--- Score

117. Has the Sales Leader work been fairly and/ or equitably divided and delegated among team members who are qualified and capable to perform the work? Has everyone contributed?
<--- Score

118. What key stakeholder process output measure(s) does Sales Leader leverage and how?
<--- Score

119. Have all of the relationships been defined properly?
<--- Score

120. Are roles and responsibilities formally defined?
<--- Score

121. Is there any additional Sales Leader definition of success?
<--- Score

122. What are the Sales Leader use cases?

<--- Score

123. How do you manage scope?
<--- Score

124. Who defines (or who defined) the rules and roles?
<--- Score

125. Are there different segments of customers?
<--- Score

126. How is the team tracking and documenting its work?
<--- Score

127. Has anyone else (internal or external to the group) attempted to solve this problem or a similar one before? If so, what knowledge can be leveraged from these previous efforts?
<--- Score

128. What is the worst case scenario?
<--- Score

129. What are the core elements of the Sales Leader business case?
<--- Score

130. How can the value of Sales Leader be defined?
<--- Score

Add up total points for this section:
_ _ _ _ _ = Total points for this section

Divided by: _ _ _ _ _ _ (number of statements answered) = _ _ _ _ _ _

Average score for this section

Transfer your score to the Sales Leader
Index at the beginning of the Self-
Assessment.

CRITERION #3: MEASURE:

INTENT: Gather the correct data. Measure the current performance and evolution of the situation.

In my belief, the answer to this question is clearly defined:

5 Strongly Agree

4 Agree

3 Neutral

2 Disagree

1 Strongly Disagree

1. How is progress measured?
<--- Score

2. How do you verify and develop ideas and innovations?
<--- Score

3. How can you manage cost down?
<--- Score

4. How will the Sales Leader data be analyzed?
<--- Score

5. What are the current costs of the Sales Leader process?
<--- Score

6. How do your measurements capture actionable Sales Leader information for use in exceeding your customers expectations and securing your customers engagement?
<--- Score

7. What are you verifying?
<--- Score

8. How is the value delivered by Sales Leader being measured?
<--- Score

9. What is the root cause(s) of the problem?
<--- Score

10. How to cause the change?
<--- Score

11. What are the strategic priorities for this year?
<--- Score

12. Do you effectively measure and reward individual and team performance?
<--- Score

13. Where is the cost?
<--- Score

14. What is an unallowable cost?
<--- Score

15. How will your organization measure success?
<--- Score

16. How frequently do you track Sales Leader measures?
<--- Score

17. Is a follow-up focused external Sales Leader review required?
<--- Score

18. How long to keep data and how to manage retention costs?
<--- Score

19. How can you reduce the costs of obtaining inputs?
<--- Score

20. Did you tackle the cause or the symptom?
<--- Score

21. Why a Sales Leader focus?
<--- Score

22. How do you verify your resources?
<--- Score

23. What would it cost to replace your technology?
<--- Score

24. How will effects be measured?
<--- Score

25. How can you measure the performance?
<--- Score

26. Are the units of measure consistent?
<--- Score

27. What are your primary costs, revenues, assets?
<--- Score

28. How sensitive must the Sales Leader strategy be to cost?
<--- Score

29. What do you measure and why?
<--- Score

30. At what cost?
<--- Score

31. How do you control the overall costs of your work processes?
<--- Score

32. What causes mismanagement?
<--- Score

33. How are costs allocated?
<--- Score

34. What measurements are being captured?
<--- Score

35. How much does it cost?
<--- Score

36. What happens if cost savings do not materialize?
<--- Score

37. Who should receive measurement reports?
<--- Score

38. What tests verify requirements?
<--- Score

39. How do you aggregate measures across priorities?
<--- Score

40. Who is involved in verifying compliance?
<--- Score

41. How do you verify performance?
<--- Score

42. Are you taking your company in the direction of better and revenue or cheaper and cost?
<--- Score

43. What are the estimated costs of proposed changes?
<--- Score

44. How is performance measured?
<--- Score

45. What are the costs and benefits?
<--- Score

46. Among the Sales Leader product and service cost to be estimated, which is considered hardest to estimate?
<--- Score

47. Are indirect costs charged to the Sales Leader program?
<--- Score

48. The approach of traditional Sales Leader works for detail complexity but is focused on a systematic approach rather than an understanding of the nature of systems themselves, what approach will permit your organization to deal with the kind of unpredictable emergent behaviors that dynamic complexity can introduce?
<--- Score

49. Are you able to realize any cost savings?
<--- Score

50. Do you have any cost Sales Leader limitation requirements?
<--- Score

51. Does the Sales Leader task fit the client's priorities?
<--- Score

52. What would be a real cause for concern?
<--- Score

53. Have design-to-cost goals been established?
<--- Score

54. Was a business case (cost/benefit) developed?
<--- Score

55. What are the costs of delaying Sales Leader action?
<--- Score

56. How can you measure Sales Leader in a systematic way?
<--- Score

57. What are hidden Sales Leader quality costs?
<--- Score

58. What is the cost of rework?
<--- Score

59. Does a Sales Leader quantification method exist?
<--- Score

60. What drives O&M cost?
<--- Score

61. What details are required of the Sales Leader cost structure?
<--- Score

62. Do you verify that corrective actions were taken?
<--- Score

63. How do you measure success?
<--- Score

64. Are there measurements based on task performance?
<--- Score

65. What does a Test Case verify?
<--- Score

66. What users will be impacted?
<--- Score

67. What evidence is there and what is measured?
<--- Score

68. Have you made assumptions about the shape of the future, particularly its impact on your customers and competitors?
<--- Score

69. Is the cost worth the Sales Leader effort ?
<--- Score

70. Are the Sales Leader benefits worth its costs?
<--- Score

71. What do people want to verify?
<--- Score

72. How can you reduce costs?
<--- Score

73. What does verifying compliance entail?
<--- Score

74. How do you verify if Sales Leader is built right?
<--- Score

75. How do you stay flexible and focused to recognize larger Sales Leader results?
<--- Score

76. Where is it measured?
<--- Score

77. What causes innovation to fail or succeed in your organization?
<--- Score

78. What harm might be caused?
<--- Score

79. What is the total fixed cost?
<--- Score

80. How do you prevent mis-estimating cost?
<--- Score

81. Has a cost center been established?
<--- Score

82. Are supply costs steady or fluctuating?
<--- Score

83. How do you verify the authenticity of the data and information used?
<--- Score

84. Where can you go to verify the info?
<--- Score

85. What is your Sales Leader quality cost segregation study?
<--- Score

86. What could cause delays in the schedule?
<--- Score

87. Which measures and indicators matter?
<--- Score

88. What are the Sales Leader key cost drivers?
<--- Score

89. How do you measure lifecycle phases?
<--- Score

90. Are there any easy-to-implement alternatives to Sales Leader? Sometimes other solutions are available that do not require the cost implications of a full-blown project?
<--- Score

91. What are the costs of reform?
<--- Score

92. What are the uncertainties surrounding estimates of impact?
<--- Score

93. What are your operating costs?
<--- Score

94. Who pays the cost?
<--- Score

95. How will measures be used to manage and adapt?
<--- Score

96. Are missed Sales Leader opportunities costing your organization money?
<--- Score

97. What could cause you to change course?
<--- Score

98. How will you measure your Sales Leader effectiveness?
<--- Score

99. How do you focus on what is right -not who is right?
<--- Score

100. What are allowable costs?
<--- Score

101. How do you verify and validate the Sales Leader data?
<--- Score

102. What are the operational costs after Sales Leader deployment?
<--- Score

103. Why do you expend time and effort to implement measurement, for whom?
<--- Score

104. How can a Sales Leader test verify your ideas or assumptions?
<--- Score

105. Why do the measurements/indicators matter?
<--- Score

106. What is measured? Why?
<--- Score

107. What causes extra work or rework?
<--- Score

108. Have you included everything in your Sales Leader cost models?
<--- Score

109. Which Sales Leader impacts are significant?
<--- Score

110. Will Sales Leader have an impact on current business continuity, disaster recovery processes and/or infrastructure?
<--- Score

111. What are the costs?
<--- Score

112. What does your operating model cost?
<--- Score

113. What is the Sales Leader business impact?
<--- Score

114. Is there an opportunity to verify requirements?
<--- Score

115. What are your key Sales Leader organizational performance measures, including key short and longer-term financial measures?
<--- Score

116. What disadvantage does this cause for the user?
<--- Score

117. How are you verifying it?
<--- Score

118. Do you have a flow diagram of what happens?
<--- Score

119. How will success or failure be measured?
<--- Score

120. How do you quantify and qualify impacts?
<--- Score

121. When are costs are incurred?
<--- Score

122. Is it possible to estimate the impact of unanticipated complexity such as wrong or failed assumptions, feedback, etcetera on proposed reforms?
<--- Score

123. Does management have the right priorities among projects?
<--- Score

124. How do you measure variability?
<--- Score

125. Are there competing Sales Leader priorities?
<--- Score

126. How are measurements made?
<--- Score

127. How will costs be allocated?
<--- Score

128. What are your customers expectations and measures?
<--- Score

129. Which costs should be taken into account?
<--- Score

130. What is the cause of any Sales Leader gaps?
<--- Score

131. What relevant entities could be measured?
<--- Score

132. What methods are feasible and acceptable to estimate the impact of reforms?
<--- Score

133. When should you bother with diagrams?
<--- Score

134. Are you aware of what could cause a problem?
<--- Score

135. Are the measurements objective?
<--- Score

136. What is the total cost related to deploying Sales Leader, including any consulting or professional services?
<--- Score

137. What measurements are possible, practicable and meaningful?
<--- Score

138. Do you have an issue in getting priority?
<--- Score

139. What does losing customers cost your organization?
<--- Score

140. What can be used to verify compliance?

<--- Score

141. Is the solution cost-effective?
<--- Score

142. Are actual costs in line with budgeted costs?
<--- Score

Add up total points for this section:
_____ = Total points for this section

Divided by: _____ (number of
statements answered) = _____
Average score for this section

Transfer your score to the Sales Leader
Index at the beginning of the Self-
Assessment.

CRITERION #4: ANALYZE:

INTENT: Analyze causes, assumptions and hypotheses.

In my belief, the answer to this question is clearly defined:

5 Strongly Agree

4 Agree

3 Neutral

2 Disagree

1 Strongly Disagree

1. Do you understand your management processes today?
<--- Score

2. What Sales Leader metrics are outputs of the process?
<--- Score

3. Do several people in different organizational units assist with the Sales Leader process?

<--- Score

4. Record-keeping requirements flow from the records needed as inputs, outputs, controls and for transformation of a Sales Leader process, are the records needed as inputs to the Sales Leader process available?
<--- Score

5. Have the problem and goal statements been updated to reflect the additional knowledge gained from the analyze phase?
<--- Score

6. Is the final output clearly identified?
<--- Score

7. What other organizational variables, such as reward systems or communication systems, affect the performance of this Sales Leader process?
<--- Score

8. Who is involved in the management review process?
<--- Score

9. What tools were used to generate the list of possible causes?
<--- Score

10. What Sales Leader data should be collected?
<--- Score

11. Do quality systems drive continuous improvement?
<--- Score

12. Do you, as a leader, bounce back quickly from setbacks?
<--- Score

13. What is the cost of poor quality as supported by the team's analysis?
<--- Score

14. How will corresponding data be collected?
<--- Score

15. Do your contracts/agreements contain data security obligations?
<--- Score

16. How was the detailed process map generated, verified, and validated?
<--- Score

17. Is the required Sales Leader data gathered?
<--- Score

18. Was a cause-and-effect diagram used to explore the different types of causes (or sources of variation)?
<--- Score

19. What does the data say about the performance of the stakeholder process?
<--- Score

20. How many input/output points does it require?
<--- Score

21. How do you use Sales Leader data and information to support organizational decision making and

innovation?

<--- Score

22. What are your key performance measures or indicators and in-process measures for the control and improvement of your Sales Leader processes?

<--- Score

23. What are the revised rough estimates of the financial savings/opportunity for Sales Leader improvements?

<--- Score

24. Identify an operational issue in your organization, for example, could a particular task be done more quickly or more efficiently by Sales Leader?

<--- Score

25. Should you invest in industry-recognized qualifications?

<--- Score

26. Who gets your output?

<--- Score

27. How are outputs preserved and protected?

<--- Score

28. Have any additional benefits been identified that will result from closing all or most of the gaps?

<--- Score

29. A compounding model resolution with available relevant data can often provide insight towards a solution methodology; which Sales Leader models, tools and techniques are necessary?

<--- Score

30. How does the organization define, manage, and improve its Sales Leader processes?
<--- Score

31. What are your best practices for minimizing Sales Leader project risk, while demonstrating incremental value and quick wins throughout the Sales Leader project lifecycle?
<--- Score

32. Can you add value to the current Sales Leader decision-making process (largely qualitative) by incorporating uncertainty modeling (more quantitative)?
<--- Score

33. Did any value-added analysis or 'lean thinking' take place to identify some of the gaps shown on the 'as is' process map?
<--- Score

34. What controls do you have in place to protect data?
<--- Score

35. Do your leaders quickly bounce back from setbacks?
<--- Score

36. When should a process be art not science?
<--- Score

37. Are all team members qualified for all tasks?
<--- Score

38. What are the Sales Leader business drivers?
<--- Score

39. What did the team gain from developing a sub-process map?
<--- Score

40. What qualifications do Sales Leader leaders need?
<--- Score

41. What kind of crime could a potential new hire have committed that would not only not disqualify him/her from being hired by your organization, but would actually indicate that he/she might be a particularly good fit?
<--- Score

42. What conclusions were drawn from the team's data collection and analysis? How did the team reach these conclusions?
<--- Score

43. What successful thing are you doing today that may be blinding you to new growth opportunities?
<--- Score

44. How do you promote understanding that opportunity for improvement is not criticism of the status quo, or the people who created the status quo?
<--- Score

45. What are your current levels and trends in key measures or indicators of Sales Leader product and process performance that are important to and directly serve your customers? How do these results

compare with the performance of your competitors and other organizations with similar offerings?
<--- Score

46. What training and qualifications will you need?
<--- Score

47. Where is the data coming from to measure compliance?
<--- Score

48. Were Pareto charts (or similar) used to portray the 'heavy hitters' (or key sources of variation)?
<--- Score

49. How is data used for program management and improvement?
<--- Score

50. What is the complexity of the output produced?
<--- Score

51. Were there any improvement opportunities identified from the process analysis?
<--- Score

52. What are the processes for audit reporting and management?
<--- Score

53. What is the Sales Leader Driver?
<--- Score

54. Was a detailed process map created to amplify critical steps of the 'as is' stakeholder process?
<--- Score

55. Do you have the authority to produce the output?
<--- Score

56. What are your Sales Leader processes?
<--- Score

57. How can risk management be tied procedurally to process elements?
<--- Score

58. What information qualified as important?
<--- Score

59. Are gaps between current performance and the goal performance identified?
<--- Score

60. Who owns what data?
<--- Score

61. What is the oversight process?
<--- Score

62. How will the change process be managed?
<--- Score

63. Where can you get qualified talent today?
<--- Score

64. What Sales Leader data will be collected?
<--- Score

65. Has an output goal been set?
<--- Score

66. Did any additional data need to be collected?
<--- Score

67. Are all staff in core Sales Leader subjects Highly Qualified?
<--- Score

68. Think about the functions involved in your Sales Leader project, what processes flow from these functions?
<--- Score

69. Are you missing Sales Leader opportunities?
<--- Score

70. How has the Sales Leader data been gathered?
<--- Score

71. What do you need to qualify?
<--- Score

72. How do you identify specific Sales Leader investment opportunities and emerging trends?
<--- Score

73. What other jobs or tasks affect the performance of the steps in the Sales Leader process?
<--- Score

74. Who qualifies to gain access to data?
<--- Score

75. Do staff qualifications match your project?
<--- Score

76. Is there an established change management

process?
<--- Score

77. What process improvements will be needed?
<--- Score

78. How do you define collaboration and team output?
<--- Score

79. What is your organizations process which leads to recognition of value generation?
<--- Score

80. How much data can be collected in the given timeframe?
<--- Score

81. What are the necessary qualifications?
<--- Score

82. How is Sales Leader data gathered?
<--- Score

83. Who will gather what data?
<--- Score

84. What were the financial benefits resulting from any 'ground fruit or low-hanging fruit' (quick fixes)?
<--- Score

85. Is the gap/opportunity displayed and communicated in financial terms?
<--- Score

86. What is the output?

<--- Score

87. What are the disruptive Sales Leader technologies that enable your organization to radically change your business processes?
<--- Score

88. Were any designed experiments used to generate additional insight into the data analysis?
<--- Score

89. What data is gathered?
<--- Score

90. Is data and process analysis, root cause analysis and quantifying the gap/opportunity in place?
<--- Score

91. Where is Sales Leader data gathered?
<--- Score

92. Do your employees have the opportunity to do what they do best everyday?
<--- Score

93. What data do you need to collect?
<--- Score

94. What were the crucial 'moments of truth' on the process map?
<--- Score

95. What will drive Sales Leader change?
<--- Score

96. What tools were used to narrow the list of possible

causes?
<--- Score

97. What Sales Leader data should be managed?
<--- Score

98. How difficult is it to qualify what Sales Leader ROI is?
<--- Score

99. What qualifications and skills do you need?
<--- Score

100. An organizationally feasible system request is one that considers the mission, goals and objectives of the organization, key questions are: is the Sales Leader solution request practical and will it solve a problem or take advantage of an opportunity to achieve company goals?
<--- Score

101. How do your work systems and key work processes relate to and capitalize on your core competencies?
<--- Score

102. Think about some of the processes you undertake within your organization, which do you own?
<--- Score

103. What are evaluation criteria for the output?
<--- Score

104. What resources go in to get the desired output?
<--- Score

105. What quality tools were used to get through the analyze phase?
<--- Score

106. Is the Sales Leader process severely broken such that a re-design is necessary?
<--- Score

107. How will the Sales Leader data be captured?
<--- Score

108. What process should you select for improvement?
<--- Score

109. What systems/processes must you excel at?
<--- Score

110. How will the data be checked for quality?
<--- Score

111. Is there a strict change management process?
<--- Score

112. What are the personnel training and qualifications required?
<--- Score

113. How is the way you as the leader think and process information affecting your organizational culture?
<--- Score

114. Who will facilitate the team and process?
<--- Score

115. What, related to, Sales Leader processes does your organization outsource?
<--- Score

116. Is pre-qualification of suppliers carried out?
<--- Score

117. How often will data be collected for measures?
<--- Score

118. What are your current levels and trends in key Sales Leader measures or indicators of product and process performance that are important to and directly serve your customers?
<--- Score

119. How do you ensure that the Sales Leader opportunity is realistic?
<--- Score

120. What internal processes need improvement?
<--- Score

121. What Sales Leader data do you gather or use now?
<--- Score

122. How do you measure the operational performance of your key work systems and processes, including productivity, cycle time, and other appropriate measures of process effectiveness, efficiency, and innovation?
<--- Score

123. How is the data gathered?

<--- Score

124. Is the suppliers process defined and controlled?
<--- Score

125. Has data output been validated?
<--- Score

126. Are Sales Leader changes recognized early
enough to be approved through the regular process?
<--- Score

127. What qualifications are needed?
<--- Score

128. What qualifies as competition?
<--- Score

129. How do mission and objectives affect the Sales
Leader processes of your organization?
<--- Score

130. What are the Sales Leader design outputs?
<--- Score

131. What output to create?
<--- Score

132. Is there any way to speed up the process?
<--- Score

133. What methods do you use to gather Sales Leader
data?
<--- Score

134. Is the performance gap determined?

<--- Score

Add up total points for this section:
_ _ _ _ _ = Total points for this section

Divided by: _ _ _ _ _ _ (number of
statements answered) = _ _ _ _ _ _
Average score for this section

Transfer your score to the Sales Leader
Index at the beginning of the Self-
Assessment.

CRITERION #5: IMPROVE:

INTENT: Develop a practical solution.
Innovate, establish and test the
solution and to measure the results.

In my belief, the answer to this
question is clearly defined:

5 Strongly Agree

4 Agree

3 Neutral

2 Disagree

1 Strongly Disagree

1. Is there a high likelihood that any
recommendations will achieve their intended results?
<--- Score

2. What do you want to improve?
<--- Score

3. How is the Sales Leader Value Stream Mapping
managed?

<--- Score

4. How do you improve productivity?
<--- Score

5. How does the team improve its work?
<--- Score

6. How will you recognize and celebrate results?
<--- Score

7. What can you do to improve?
<--- Score

8. How can you better manage risk?
<--- Score

9. What practices helps your organization to develop its capacity to recognize patterns?
<--- Score

10. What assumptions are made about the solution and approach?
<--- Score

11. How are policy decisions made and where?
<--- Score

12. Who manages Sales Leader risk?
<--- Score

13. Who will be using the results of the measurement activities?
<--- Score

14. How can you improve Sales Leader?

<--- Score

15. How significant is the improvement in the eyes of the end user?
<--- Score

16. Risk events: what are the things that could go wrong?
<--- Score

17. Are you assessing Sales Leader and risk?
<--- Score

18. What is the Sales Leader's sustainability risk?
<--- Score

19. In the past few months, what is the smallest change you have made that has had the biggest positive result? What was it about that small change that produced the large return?
<--- Score

20. How will you know when its improved?
<--- Score

21. Which Sales Leader solution is appropriate?
<--- Score

22. Do vendor agreements bring new compliance risk ?
<--- Score

23. Have you achieved Sales Leader improvements?
<--- Score

24. What risks do you need to manage?

<--- Score

25. Who makes the Sales Leader decisions in your organization?
<--- Score

26. How are Sales Leader risks managed?
<--- Score

27. To what extent does management recognize Sales Leader as a tool to increase the results?
<--- Score

28. What tools were used to evaluate the potential solutions?
<--- Score

29. Who do you report Sales Leader results to?
<--- Score

30. How risky is your organization?
<--- Score

31. How will you measure the results?
<--- Score

32. What lessons, if any, from a pilot were incorporated into the design of the full-scale solution?
<--- Score

33. How do you improve your likelihood of success ?
<--- Score

34. What current systems have to be understood and/or changed?
<--- Score

35. Would you develop a Sales Leader Communication Strategy?
<--- Score

36. How do you measure progress and evaluate training effectiveness?
<--- Score

37. How can you improve performance?
<--- Score

38. What are the Sales Leader security risks?
<--- Score

39. What is the risk?
<--- Score

40. Is supporting Sales Leader documentation required?
<--- Score

41. How do you decide how much to remunerate an employee?
<--- Score

42. What are the concrete Sales Leader results?
<--- Score

43. What is Sales Leader risk?
<--- Score

44. Where do the Sales Leader decisions reside?
<--- Score

45. If you could go back in time five years, what

decision would you make differently? What is your best guess as to what decision you're making today you might regret five years from now?
<--- Score

46. What is the magnitude of the improvements?
<--- Score

47. How is knowledge sharing about risk management improved?
<--- Score

48. Where do you need Sales Leader improvement?
<--- Score

49. Why improve in the first place?
<--- Score

50. How is continuous improvement applied to risk management?
<--- Score

51. What resources are required for the improvement efforts?
<--- Score

52. What went well, what should change, what can improve?
<--- Score

53. What area needs the greatest improvement?
<--- Score

54. How do you measure improved Sales Leader service perception, and satisfaction?
<--- Score

55. What tools were most useful during the improve phase?
<--- Score

56. Do the viable solutions scale to future needs?
<--- Score

57. Sales Leader risk decisions: whose call Is It?
<--- Score

58. Is Sales Leader documentation maintained?
<--- Score

59. Is any Sales Leader documentation required?
<--- Score

60. Which of the recognised risks out of all risks can be most likely transferred?
<--- Score

61. When you map the key players in your own work and the types/domains of relationships with them, which relationships do you find easy and which challenging, and why?
<--- Score

62. How does your organization evaluate strategic Sales Leader success?
<--- Score

63. How do you improve Sales Leader service perception, and satisfaction?
<--- Score

64. Are the risks fully understood, reasonable and

manageable?
<--- Score

65. Will the controls trigger any other risks?
<--- Score

66. Is the Sales Leader solution sustainable?
<--- Score

67. Risk factors: what are the characteristics of Sales Leader that make it risky?
<--- Score

68. Can you integrate quality management and risk management?
<--- Score

69. What tools do you use once you have decided on a Sales Leader strategy and more importantly how do you choose?
<--- Score

70. Have you identified breakpoints and/or risk tolerances that will trigger broad consideration of a potential need for intervention or modification of strategy?
<--- Score

71. Who should make the Sales Leader decisions?
<--- Score

72. Are the most efficient solutions problem-specific?
<--- Score

73. Was a Sales Leader charter developed?
<--- Score

74. Explorations of the frontiers of Sales Leader will help you build influence, improve Sales Leader, optimize decision making, and sustain change, what is your approach?
<--- Score

75. Is risk periodically assessed?
<--- Score

76. Does a good decision guarantee a good outcome?
<--- Score

77. What should a proof of concept or pilot accomplish?
<--- Score

78. Do those selected for the Sales Leader team have a good general understanding of what Sales Leader is all about?
<--- Score

79. Are the key business and technology risks being managed?
<--- Score

80. Risk Identification: What are the possible risk events your organization faces in relation to Sales Leader?
<--- Score

81. What are the expected Sales Leader results?
<--- Score

82. What were the criteria for evaluating a Sales Leader pilot?

<--- Score

83. Who controls key decisions that will be made?
<--- Score

84. What needs improvement? Why?
<--- Score

85. Who are the Sales Leader decision-makers?
<--- Score

86. For decision problems, how do you develop a decision statement?
<--- Score

87. Are decisions made in a timely manner?
<--- Score

88. How do you manage and improve your Sales Leader work systems to deliver customer value and achieve organizational success and sustainability?
<--- Score

89. Do you have the optimal project management team structure?
<--- Score

90. At what point will vulnerability assessments be performed once Sales Leader is put into production (e.g., ongoing Risk Management after implementation)?
<--- Score

91. What tools were used to tap into the creativity and encourage 'outside the box' thinking?
<--- Score

92. Are procedures documented for managing Sales Leader risks?
<--- Score

93. Who will be responsible for documenting the Sales Leader requirements in detail?
<--- Score

94. Can the solution be designed and implemented within an acceptable time period?
<--- Score

95. Who are the Sales Leader decision makers?
<--- Score

96. What criteria will you use to assess your Sales Leader risks?
<--- Score

97. What improvements have been achieved?
<--- Score

98. How do the Sales Leader results compare with the performance of your competitors and other organizations with similar offerings?
<--- Score

99. Does the goal represent a desired result that can be measured?
<--- Score

100. Is there any other Sales Leader solution?
<--- Score

101. Are events managed to resolution?

<--- Score

102. Is the Sales Leader documentation thorough?
<--- Score

103. How scalable is your Sales Leader solution?
<--- Score

104. Is the measure of success for Sales Leader understandable to a variety of people?
<--- Score

105. How do you deal with Sales Leader risk?
<--- Score

106. Is the Sales Leader risk managed?
<--- Score

107. How do you go about comparing Sales Leader approaches/solutions?
<--- Score

108. For estimation problems, how do you develop an estimation statement?
<--- Score

109. Do you need to do a usability evaluation?
<--- Score

110. What were the underlying assumptions on the cost-benefit analysis?
<--- Score

111. How do you measure risk?
<--- Score

112. Who are the people involved in developing and implementing Sales Leader?
<--- Score

113. Is the solution technically practical?
<--- Score

114. What are the implications of the one critical Sales Leader decision 10 minutes, 10 months, and 10 years from now?
<--- Score

115. How do you mitigate Sales Leader risk?
<--- Score

116. Who manages supplier risk management in your organization?
<--- Score

117. What Sales Leader improvements can be made?
<--- Score

118. What are the affordable Sales Leader risks?
<--- Score

119. How can the phases of Sales Leader development be identified?
<--- Score

120. What are your current levels and trends in key measures or indicators of workforce and leader development?
<--- Score

121. Are risk triggers captured?
<--- Score

122. Do you combine technical expertise with business knowledge and Sales Leader Key topics include lifecycles, development approaches, requirements and how to make a business case?
<--- Score

123. What alternative responses are available to manage risk?
<--- Score

124. How do you manage Sales Leader risk?
<--- Score

125. How do you define the solutions' scope?
<--- Score

126. Who controls the risk?
<--- Score

127. How will you know that a change is an improvement?
<--- Score

128. What actually has to improve and by how much?
<--- Score

129. What to do with the results or outcomes of measurements?
<--- Score

130. What strategies for Sales Leader improvement are successful?
<--- Score

131. Are risk management tasks balanced centrally

and locally?
<--- Score

Add up total points for this section:
_ _ _ _ _ = Total points for this section

Divided by: _ _ _ _ _ _ (number of
statements answered) = _ _ _ _ _ _
Average score for this section

Transfer your score to the Sales Leader
Index at the beginning of the Self-
Assessment.

CRITERION #6: CONTROL:

INTENT: Implement the practical solution. Maintain the performance and correct possible complications.

In my belief, the answer to this question is clearly defined:

5 Strongly Agree

4 Agree

3 Neutral

2 Disagree

1 Strongly Disagree

1. Who sets the Sales Leader standards?
<--- Score

2. How do you spread information?
<--- Score

3. How will the process owner and team be able to hold the gains?
<--- Score

4. Where do ideas that reach policy makers and planners as proposals for Sales Leader strengthening and reform actually originate?
<--- Score

5. Are documented procedures clear and easy to follow for the operators?
<--- Score

6. Who will be in control?
<--- Score

7. Are the Sales Leader standards challenging?
<--- Score

8. How likely is the current Sales Leader plan to come in on schedule or on budget?
<--- Score

9. Is there documentation that will support the successful operation of the improvement?
<--- Score

10. Is there a standardized process?
<--- Score

11. What Sales Leader standards are applicable?
<--- Score

12. Will any special training be provided for results interpretation?
<--- Score

13. Is knowledge gained on process shared and institutionalized?

<--- Score

14. Against what alternative is success being measured?
<--- Score

15. Who is going to spread your message?
<--- Score

16. Is there a recommended audit plan for routine surveillance inspections of Sales Leader's gains?
<--- Score

17. How is Sales Leader project cost planned, managed, monitored?
<--- Score

18. Are there documented procedures?
<--- Score

19. What should you measure to verify efficiency gains?
<--- Score

20. Does the response plan contain a definite closed loop continual improvement scheme (e.g., plan-do-check-act)?
<--- Score

21. In the case of a Sales Leader project, the criteria for the audit derive from implementation objectives, an audit of a Sales Leader project involves assessing whether the recommendations outlined for implementation have been met, can you track that any Sales Leader project is implemented as planned, and is it working?

<--- Score

22. How will the day-to-day responsibilities for monitoring and continual improvement be transferred from the improvement team to the process owner?
<--- Score

23. Will existing staff require re-training, for example, to learn new business processes?
<--- Score

24. Does Sales Leader appropriately measure and monitor risk?
<--- Score

25. What are the critical parameters to watch?
<--- Score

26. Are pertinent alerts monitored, analyzed and distributed to appropriate personnel?
<--- Score

27. Will the team be available to assist members in planning investigations?
<--- Score

28. What are you attempting to measure/monitor?
<--- Score

29. What is the control/monitoring plan?
<--- Score

30. Does a troubleshooting guide exist or is it needed?
<--- Score

31. How will new or emerging customer needs/
requirements be checked/communicated to orient
the process toward meeting the new specifications
and continually reducing variation?
<--- Score

32. What is your theory of human motivation, and
how does your compensation plan fit with that view?
<--- Score

33. How do you plan for the cost of succession?
<--- Score

34. Are suggested corrective/restorative actions
indicated on the response plan for known causes to
problems that might surface?
<--- Score

35. What do you stand for--and what are you against?
<--- Score

36. What is the recommended frequency of auditing?
<--- Score

37. Is a response plan in place for when the input,
process, or output measures indicate an 'out-of-
control' condition?
<--- Score

38. How widespread is its use?
<--- Score

39. How do you encourage people to take control and
responsibility?
<--- Score

40. How can you best use all of your knowledge repositories to enhance learning and sharing?
<--- Score

41. What are your results for key measures or indicators of the accomplishment of your Sales Leader strategy and action plans, including building and strengthening core competencies?
<--- Score

42. Are operating procedures consistent?
<--- Score

43. Who is the Sales Leader process owner?
<--- Score

44. What are customers monitoring?
<--- Score

45. Are new process steps, standards, and documentation ingrained into normal operations?
<--- Score

46. Can support from partners be adjusted?
<--- Score

47. What adjustments to the strategies are needed?
<--- Score

48. What is your plan to assess your security risks?
<--- Score

49. What are the key elements of your Sales Leader performance improvement system, including your evaluation, organizational learning, and innovation processes?

<--- Score

50. What key inputs and outputs are being measured on an ongoing basis?
<--- Score

51. How do you monitor usage and cost?
<--- Score

52. Do you monitor the Sales Leader decisions made and fine tune them as they evolve?
<--- Score

53. How might the group capture best practices and lessons learned so as to leverage improvements?
<--- Score

54. How will Sales Leader decisions be made and monitored?
<--- Score

55. What is the standard for acceptable Sales Leader performance?
<--- Score

56. How will report readings be checked to effectively monitor performance?
<--- Score

57. Implementation Planning: is a pilot needed to test the changes before a full roll out occurs?
<--- Score

58. What quality tools were useful in the control phase?
<--- Score

59. Do you monitor the effectiveness of your Sales Leader activities?
<--- Score

60. How will the process owner verify improvement in present and future sigma levels, process capabilities?
<--- Score

61. Has the Sales Leader value of standards been quantified?
<--- Score

62. Is new knowledge gained imbedded in the response plan?
<--- Score

63. Can you adapt and adjust to changing Sales Leader situations?
<--- Score

64. Does job training on the documented procedures need to be part of the process team's education and training?
<--- Score

65. Do the Sales Leader decisions you make today help people and the planet tomorrow?
<--- Score

66. How is change control managed?
<--- Score

67. Are you measuring, monitoring and predicting Sales Leader activities to optimize operations and profitability, and enhancing outcomes?

<--- Score

68. Are the planned controls working?
<--- Score

69. What other areas of the group might benefit from the Sales Leader team's improvements, knowledge, and learning?
<--- Score

70. What should the next improvement project be that is related to Sales Leader?
<--- Score

71. Act/Adjust: What Do you Need to Do Differently?
<--- Score

72. How do controls support value?
<--- Score

73. You may have created your quality measures at a time when you lacked resources, technology wasn't up to the required standard, or low service levels were the industry norm. Have those circumstances changed?
<--- Score

74. Is there a control plan in place for sustaining improvements (short and long-term)?
<--- Score

75. What other systems, operations, processes, and infrastructures (hiring practices, staffing, training, incentives/rewards, metrics/dashboards/scorecards, etc.) need updates, additions, changes, or deletions in order to facilitate knowledge transfer and

improvements?
<--- Score

76. What can you control?
<--- Score

77. How do you establish and deploy modified action plans if circumstances require a shift in plans and rapid execution of new plans?
<--- Score

78. How will input, process, and output variables be checked to detect for sub-optimal conditions?
<--- Score

79. How do senior leaders actions reflect a commitment to the organizations Sales Leader values?
<--- Score

80. What is the best design framework for Sales Leader organization now that, in a post industrial-age if the top-down, command and control model is no longer relevant?
<--- Score

81. Is there a transfer of ownership and knowledge to process owner and process team tasked with the responsibilities.
<--- Score

82. How do your controls stack up?
<--- Score

83. Has the improved process and its steps been standardized?

<--- Score

84. What do your reports reflect?
<--- Score

85. Does the Sales Leader performance meet the customer's requirements?
<--- Score

86. What do you measure to verify effectiveness gains?
<--- Score

87. Is there a Sales Leader Communication plan covering who needs to get what information when?
<--- Score

88. Is a response plan established and deployed?
<--- Score

89. Is reporting being used or needed?
<--- Score

90. Who has control over resources?
<--- Score

91. How will you measure your QA plan's effectiveness?
<--- Score

92. Is there a documented and implemented monitoring plan?
<--- Score

93. Who controls critical resources?
<--- Score

94. Have new or revised work instructions resulted?
<--- Score

95. Are controls in place and consistently applied?
<--- Score

96. Are the planned controls in place?
<--- Score

97. Is the Sales Leader test/monitoring cost justified?
<--- Score

Add up total points for this section:
_ _ _ _ _ = Total points for this section

Divided by: _ _ _ _ _ _ (number of
statements answered) = _ _ _ _ _ _
Average score for this section

Transfer your score to the Sales Leader
Index at the beginning of the Self-
Assessment.

CRITERION #7: SUSTAIN:

INTENT: Retain the benefits.

In my belief, the answer to this question is clearly defined:

5 Strongly Agree

4 Agree

3 Neutral

2 Disagree

1 Strongly Disagree

1. Is maximizing Sales Leader protection the same as minimizing Sales Leader loss?
<--- Score

2. Is your basic point _____ or _____?
<--- Score

3. How do you keep the momentum going?
<--- Score

4. Are you paying enough attention to the partners

your company depends on to succeed?
<--- Score

5. How do you go about securing Sales Leader?
<--- Score

6. What is your competitive advantage?
<--- Score

7. Which models, tools and techniques are necessary?
<--- Score

8. How do you manage Sales Leader Knowledge
Management (KM)?
<--- Score

9. What are the long-term Sales Leader goals?
<--- Score

10. Instead of going to current contacts for new ideas,
what if you reconnected with dormant contacts--
the people you used to know? If you were going
reactivate a dormant tie, who would it be?
<--- Score

11. How do you track customer value, profitability
or financial return, organizational success, and
sustainability?
<--- Score

12. Is a Sales Leader team work effort in place?
<--- Score

13. Who is responsible for ensuring appropriate
resources (time, people and money) are allocated to
Sales Leader?

<--- Score

14. Is there any reason to believe the opposite of my current belief?
<--- Score

15. Who are the key stakeholders?
<--- Score

16. Who uses your product in ways you never expected?
<--- Score

17. What is the overall business strategy?
<--- Score

18. How do you accomplish your long range Sales Leader goals?
<--- Score

19. Operational - will it work?
<--- Score

20. What stupid rule would you most like to kill?
<--- Score

21. Can you do all this work?
<--- Score

22. To whom do you add value?
<--- Score

23. How many sales leaders have failed?
<--- Score

24. What could happen if you do not do it?

<--- Score

25. What are the short and long-term Sales Leader goals?
<--- Score

26. What are the success criteria that will indicate that Sales Leader objectives have been met and the benefits delivered?
<--- Score

27. Why is Sales Leader important for you now?
<--- Score

28. What is the recommended frequency of auditing?
<--- Score

29. How do you foster the skills, knowledge, talents, attributes, and characteristics you want to have?
<--- Score

30. What happens at your organization when people fail?
<--- Score

31. What is effective Sales Leader?
<--- Score

32. Which Sales Leader goals are the most important?
<--- Score

33. Is the Sales Leader organization completing tasks effectively and efficiently?
<--- Score

34. Do you have enough freaky customers in your

portfolio pushing you to the limit day in and day out?
<--- Score

35. How much have failed sales leaders lost?
<--- Score

36. What is something you believe that nearly no one agrees with you on?
<--- Score

37. How much contingency will be available in the budget?
<--- Score

38. How can you become the company that would put you out of business?
<--- Score

39. How much does Sales Leader help?
<--- Score

40. Will it be accepted by users?
<--- Score

41. Do you see more potential in people than they do in themselves?
<--- Score

42. Political -is anyone trying to undermine this project?
<--- Score

43. What new services of functionality will be implemented next with Sales Leader ?
<--- Score

44. What is the purpose of Sales Leader in relation to the mission?
<--- Score

45. If you had to leave your organization for a year and the only communication you could have with employees/colleagues was a single paragraph, what would you write?
<--- Score

46. Why not do Sales Leader?
<--- Score

47. What is the funding source for this project?
<--- Score

48. Are your responses positive or negative?
<--- Score

49. What are internal and external Sales Leader relations?
<--- Score

50. Think of your Sales Leader project, what are the main functions?
<--- Score

51. What is the overall talent health of your organization as a whole at senior levels, and for each organization reporting to a member of the Senior Leadership Team?
<--- Score

52. Who is responsible for Sales Leader?
<--- Score

53. How does Sales Leader integrate with other stakeholder initiatives?
<--- Score

54. Can the schedule be done in the given time?
<--- Score

55. What are the rules and assumptions your industry operates under? What if the opposite were true?
<--- Score

56. Is Sales Leader dependent on the successful delivery of a current project?
<--- Score

57. What are the gaps in your knowledge and experience?
<--- Score

58. Do you know who is a friend or a foe?
<--- Score

59. In the past year, what have you done (or could you have done) to increase the accurate perception of your company/brand as ethical and honest?
<--- Score

60. What goals did you miss?
<--- Score

61. How are you doing compared to your industry?
<--- Score

62. How do you assess the Sales Leader pitfalls that are inherent in implementing it?
<--- Score

63. Do you have the right people on the bus?
<--- Score

64. How do you engage the workforce, in addition to satisfying them?
<--- Score

65. Is your strategy driving your strategy? Or is the way in which you allocate resources driving your strategy?
<--- Score

66. How do customers see your organization?
<--- Score

67. What is your BATNA (best alternative to a negotiated agreement)?
<--- Score

68. What is it like to work for you?
<--- Score

69. What you are going to do to affect the numbers?
<--- Score

70. Who do you think the world wants your organization to be?
<--- Score

71. Who is on the team?
<--- Score

72. Why will customers want to buy your organizations products/services?
<--- Score

73. How likely is it that a customer would recommend your company to a friend or colleague?
<--- Score

74. How do senior leaders deploy your organizations vision and values through your leadership system, to the workforce, to key suppliers and partners, and to customers and other stakeholders, as appropriate?
<--- Score

75. What trouble can you get into?
<--- Score

76. What are your most important goals for the strategic Sales Leader objectives?
<--- Score

77. How do you deal with Sales Leader changes?
<--- Score

78. If you had to rebuild your organization without any traditional competitive advantages (i.e., no killer technology, promising research, innovative product/ service delivery model, etcetera), how would your people have to approach their work and collaborate together in order to create the necessary conditions for success?
<--- Score

79. Marketing budgets are tighter, consumers are more skeptical, and social media has changed forever the way we talk about Sales Leader, how do you gain traction?
<--- Score

80. What Sales Leader skills are most important?
<--- Score

81. Who will determine interim and final deadlines?
<--- Score

82. What are the challenges?
<--- Score

83. How do you cross-sell and up-sell your Sales Leader success?
<--- Score

84. What are the top 3 things at the forefront of your Sales Leader agendas for the next 3 years?
<--- Score

85. Do you have the right customers?
<--- Score

86. Is a Sales Leader breakthrough on the horizon?
<--- Score

87. What projects are going on in the organization today, and what resources are those projects using from the resource pools?
<--- Score

88. Why should people listen to you?
<--- Score

89. What is the big Sales Leader idea?
<--- Score

90. Whom among your colleagues do you trust, and for what?

<--- Score

91. What would have to be true for the option on the table to be the best possible choice?
<--- Score

92. If no one would ever find out about your accomplishments, how would you lead differently?
<--- Score

93. Do you think you know, or do you know you know ?
<--- Score

94. How do you foster innovation?
<--- Score

95. Are all key stakeholders present at all Structured Walkthroughs?
<--- Score

96. How do you transition from the baseline to the target?
<--- Score

97. What did you miss in the interview for the worst hire you ever made?
<--- Score

98. What have been your experiences in defining long range Sales Leader goals?
<--- Score

99. How will you motivate the stakeholders with the least vested interest?
<--- Score

100. What is the estimated value of the project?
<--- Score

101. What management system can you use to leverage the Sales Leader experience, ideas, and concerns of the people closest to the work to be done?
<--- Score

102. Is Sales Leader realistic, or are you setting yourself up for failure?
<--- Score

103. Can you break it down?
<--- Score

104. What trophy do you want on your mantle?
<--- Score

105. What happens when a new employee joins the organization?
<--- Score

106. What are the business goals Sales Leader is aiming to achieve?
<--- Score

107. Can you maintain your growth without detracting from the factors that have contributed to your success?
<--- Score

108. In a project to restructure Sales Leader outcomes, which stakeholders would you involve?
<--- Score

109. What is your question? Why?
<--- Score

110. What may be the consequences for the performance of an organization if all stakeholders are not consulted regarding Sales Leader?
<--- Score

111. How do you stay inspired?
<--- Score

112. How can you negotiate Sales Leader successfully with a stubborn boss, an irate client, or a deceitful coworker?
<--- Score

113. Why do and why don't your customers like your organization?
<--- Score

114. What are the key enablers to make this Sales Leader move?
<--- Score

115. How is implementation research currently incorporated into each of your goals?
<--- Score

116. Who have you, as a company, historically been when you've been at your best?
<--- Score

117. Who will be responsible for deciding whether Sales Leader goes ahead or not after the initial investigations?

<--- Score

118. What information is critical to your organization that your executives are ignoring?
<--- Score

119. How can you incorporate support to ensure safe and effective use of Sales Leader into the services that you provide?
<--- Score

120. What Sales Leader modifications can you make work for you?
<--- Score

121. Is it economical; do you have the time and money?
<--- Score

122. What do we do when new problems arise?
<--- Score

123. Is there any existing Sales Leader governance structure?
<--- Score

124. Why should you adopt a Sales Leader framework?
<--- Score

125. Do you have the right capabilities and capacities?
<--- Score

126. How do you set Sales Leader stretch targets and how do you get people to not only participate in setting these stretch targets but also that they strive to achieve these?

<--- Score

127. Has implementation been effective in reaching specified objectives so far?
<--- Score

128. What counts that you are not counting?
<--- Score

129. What relationships among Sales Leader trends do you perceive?
<--- Score

130. What is the craziest thing you can do?
<--- Score

131. What is an unauthorized commitment?
<--- Score

132. How do you make the shift from operational sales management to becoming a strategic sales leader?
<--- Score

133. How do you create buy-in?
<--- Score

134. How long will it take to change?
<--- Score

135. Are you making progress, and are you making progress as Sales Leader leaders?
<--- Score

136. Are assumptions made in Sales Leader stated explicitly?

<--- Score

137. What are the potential basics of Sales Leader fraud?
<--- Score

138. Did your employees make progress today?
<--- Score

139. What are the barriers to increased Sales Leader production?
<--- Score

140. How will you ensure you get what you expected?
<--- Score

141. What potential megatrends could make your business model obsolete?
<--- Score

142. Why is it important to have senior management support for a Sales Leader project?
<--- Score

143. Are the criteria for selecting recommendations stated?
<--- Score

144. Have new benefits been realized?
<--- Score

145. If your company went out of business tomorrow, would anyone who doesn't get a paycheck here care?
<--- Score

146. Whose voice (department, ethnic group, women,

older workers, etc) might you have missed hearing from in your company, and how might you amplify this voice to create positive momentum for your business?
<--- Score

147. What was the last experiment you ran?
<--- Score

148. Do you feel that more should be done in the Sales Leader area?
<--- Score

149. Are the assumptions believable and achievable?
<--- Score

150. Who is responsible for errors?
<--- Score

151. What are you trying to prove to yourself, and how might it be hijacking your life and business success?
<--- Score

152. Is the impact that Sales Leader has shown?
<--- Score

153. Are you maintaining a past–present–future perspective throughout the Sales Leader discussion?
<--- Score

154. In retrospect, of the projects that you pulled the plug on, what percent do you wish had been allowed to keep going, and what percent do you wish had ended earlier?
<--- Score

155. What is your formula for success in Sales Leader ?
<--- Score

156. How do you listen to customers to obtain actionable information?
<--- Score

157. Are you satisfied with your current role? If not, what is missing from it?
<--- Score

158. How do you make it meaningful in connecting Sales Leader with what users do day-to-day?
<--- Score

159. If you were responsible for initiating and implementing major changes in your organization, what steps might you take to ensure acceptance of those changes?
<--- Score

160. How do you proactively clarify deliverables and Sales Leader quality expectations?
<--- Score

161. What are strategies for increasing support and reducing opposition?
<--- Score

162. What are current Sales Leader paradigms?
<--- Score

163. If there were zero limitations, what would you do differently?
<--- Score

164. Were lessons learned captured and communicated?
<--- Score

165. What are specific Sales Leader rules to follow?
<--- Score

166. Would you rather sell to knowledgeable and informed customers or to uninformed customers?
<--- Score

167. Are new benefits received and understood?
<--- Score

168. What are the essentials of internal Sales Leader management?
<--- Score

169. What are your personal philosophies regarding Sales Leader and how do they influence your work?
<--- Score

170. Do you say no to customers for no reason?
<--- Score

171. How will you know that the Sales Leader project has been successful?
<--- Score

172. Which individuals, teams or departments will be involved in Sales Leader?
<--- Score

173. What is the source of the strategies for Sales Leader strengthening and reform?
<--- Score

174. Are you relevant? Will you be relevant five years from now? Ten?
<--- Score

175. If you do not follow, then how to lead?
<--- Score

176. Who will provide the final approval of Sales Leader deliverables?
<--- Score

177. What is the range of capabilities?
<--- Score

178. What threat is Sales Leader addressing?
<--- Score

179. Ask: what is the ratio of new Sales Leaders to new distributors?
<--- Score

180. How important is Sales Leader to the user organizations mission?
<--- Score

181. How do you maintain Sales Leader's Integrity?
<--- Score

182. At what moment would you think; Will I get fired?
<--- Score

183. What must you excel at?
<--- Score

184. Will there be any necessary staff changes

(redundancies or new hires)?
<--- Score

185. Do you have an implicit bias for capital investments over people investments?
<--- Score

186. How many sales leaders ask themselves: do you have the right customers?
<--- Score

187. What is a feasible sequencing of reform initiatives over time?
<--- Score

188. How do you know if you are successful?
<--- Score

189. Who are four people whose careers you have enhanced?
<--- Score

190. What are the usability implications of Sales Leader actions?
<--- Score

191. Who is the main stakeholder, with ultimate responsibility for driving Sales Leader forward?
<--- Score

192. Are you / should you be revolutionary or evolutionary?
<--- Score

193. Who do we want your customers to become?
<--- Score

194. Which functions and people interact with the supplier and or customer?
<--- Score

195. What should you stop doing?
<--- Score

196. Have benefits been optimized with all key stakeholders?
<--- Score

197. How do you determine the key elements that affect Sales Leader workforce satisfaction, how are these elements determined for different workforce groups and segments?
<--- Score

198. Do you know what you are doing? And who do you call if you don't?
<--- Score

199. What happens if you do not have enough funding?
<--- Score

200. Do Sales Leader rules make a reasonable demand on a users capabilities?
<--- Score

201. Do you have past Sales Leader successes?
<--- Score

202. How do you lead with Sales Leader in mind?
<--- Score

203. What would you recommend your friend do if he/she were facing this dilemma?
<--- Score

204. Who do you want your customers to become?
<--- Score

205. What unique value proposition (UVP) do you offer?
<--- Score

206. What business benefits will Sales Leader goals deliver if achieved?
<--- Score

207. What are you challenging?
<--- Score

208. If you got fired and a new hire took your place, what would she do different?
<--- Score

209. If your customer were your grandmother, would you tell her to buy what you're selling?
<--- Score

210. Ask yourself: how would you do this work if you only had one staff member to do it?
<--- Score

211. Where can you break convention?
<--- Score

212. What will be the consequences to the stakeholder (financial, reputation etc) if Sales Leader does not go ahead or fails to deliver the objectives?

<--- Score

213. If you weren't already in this business, would you enter it today? And if not, what are you going to do about it?
<--- Score

214. If you find that you havent accomplished one of the goals for one of the steps of the Sales Leader strategy, what will you do to fix it?
<--- Score

215. Who will manage the integration of tools?
<--- Score

216. Do you think Sales Leader accomplishes the goals you expect it to accomplish?
<--- Score

217. What have you done to protect your business from competitive encroachment?
<--- Score

218. Who are your customers?
<--- Score

219. How do you provide a safe environment -physically and emotionally?
<--- Score

220. How can you become more high-tech but still be high touch?
<--- Score

Add up total points for this section:
_ _ _ _ _ = Total points for this section

Divided by: _____ (number of
statements answered) = _____
Average score for this section

Transfer your score to the Sales Leader
Index at the beginning of the Self-
Assessment.

Sales Leader and Managing Projects, Criteria for Project Managers:

1.0 Initiating Process Group: Sales Leader

1. Does the Sales Leader project team have enough people to execute the Sales Leader project plan?

2. Did you use a contractor or vendor?

3. Do you know all the stakeholders impacted by the Sales Leader project and what needs are?

4. How will it affect me?

5. What must be done?

6. Did the Sales Leader project team have the right skills?

7. Realistic - are the desired results expressed in a way that the team will be motivated and believe that the required level of involvement will be obtained?

8. What areas were overlooked on this Sales Leader project?

9. Information sharing?

10. What do they need to know about the Sales Leader project?

11. If the risk event occurs, what will you do?

12. What were things that you need to improve?

13. Are there resources to maintain and support the

outcome of the Sales Leader project?

14. Measurable - are the targets measurable?

15. How well did you do?

16. Where must it be done?

17. Do you understand the communication expectations for this Sales Leader project?

18. Who is funding the Sales Leader project?

19. When are the deliverables to be generated in each phase?

20. What is the NEXT thing to do?

1.1 Project Charter: Sales Leader

21. What is the justification?

22. What is the purpose of the Sales Leader project?

23. Sales Leader project objective statement: what must the Sales Leader project do?

24. What are the deliverables?

25. Why is it important?

26. What material?

27. Strategic fit: what is the strategic initiative identifier for this Sales Leader project?

28. Why have you chosen the aim you have set forth?

29. Is it an improvement over existing products?

30. When?

31. When will this occur?

32. Is time of the essence?

33. Who ise input and support will this Sales Leader project require?

34. Must Have?

35. Run it as as a startup?

36. For whom?

37. Why is a Sales Leader project Charter used?

38. Market – identify products market, including whether it is outside of the objective: what is the purpose of the program or Sales Leader project?

39. What ideas do you have for initial tests of change (PDSA cycles)?

1.2 Stakeholder Register: Sales Leader

40. What opportunities exist to provide communications?

41. Is your organization ready for change?

42. How much influence do they have on the Sales Leader project?

43. What & Why?

44. How should employers make voices heard?

45. What is the power of the stakeholder?

46. What are the major Sales Leader project milestones requiring communications or providing communications opportunities?

47. How will reports be created?

48. Who wants to talk about Security?

49. Who is managing stakeholder engagement?

50. Who are the stakeholders?

51. How big is the gap?

1.3 Stakeholder Analysis Matrix: Sales Leader

52. What is the stakeholders name, what is function?

53. Resources, assets, people?

54. Competitor intentions - various?

55. Who is most dependent on the resources at stake?

56. What makes a person a stakeholder?

57. Which conditions out of the control of the management are crucial for the sustainability of its effects?

58. Who is directly responsible for decisions on issues important to the Sales Leader project?

59. How do customers express needs?

60. Inoculations or payment to receive them?

61. Market demand?

62. If the baseline is now, and if its improved it will be better than now?

63. Who can contribute financial or technical resources towards the work?

64. Volumes, production, economies?

65. It developments?

66. What organizational arrangements are planned to ensure the Sales Leader project achieves its social development outcomes?

67. What do you need to appraise?

68. Economy - home, abroad?

69. Which resources are required?

2.0 Planning Process Group: Sales Leader

70. What is involved in Sales Leader project scope management, and why is good Sales Leader project scope management so important on information technology Sales Leader projects?

71. How can you make your needs known?

72. Have more efficient (sensitive) and appropriate measures been adopted to respond to the political and socio-cultural problems identified?

73. How will you know you did it?

74. How well do the team follow the chosen processes?

75. Just how important is your work to the overall success of the Sales Leader project?

76. What is the critical path for this Sales Leader project, and what is the duration of the critical path?

77. Does the program have follow-up mechanisms (to verify the quality of the products, punctuality of delivery, etc.) to measure progress in the achievement of the envisaged results?

78. In what ways can the governance of the Sales Leader project be improved so that it has greater likelihood of achieving future sustainability?

79. How are the principles of aid effectiveness (ownership, alignment, management for development results and mutual responsibility) being applied in the Sales Leader project?

80. Are the follow-up indicators relevant and do they meet the quality needed to measure the outputs and outcomes of the Sales Leader project?

81. What should you do next?

82. How will you do it?

83. How well will the chosen processes produce the expected results?

84. You are creating your WBS and find that you keep decomposing tasks into smaller and smaller units. How can you tell when you are done?

85. Why is it important to determine activity sequencing on Sales Leader projects?

86. Have operating capacities been created and/or reinforced in partners?

87. Are there efficient coordination mechanisms to avoid overloading the counterparts, participating stakeholders?

88. To what extent is the program helping to influence your organizations policy framework?

2.1 Project Management Plan: Sales Leader

89. Do the proposed changes from the Sales Leader project include any significant risks to safety?

90. Are alternatives safe, functional, constructible, economical, reasonable and sustainable?

91. Are there any windfall benefits that would accrue to the Sales Leader project sponsor or other parties?

92. What did not work so well?

93. Is the budget realistic?

94. What are the assumptions?

95. What would you do differently what did not work?

96. What worked well?

97. How do you manage integration?

98. What are the known stakeholder requirements?

99. Are there any scope changes proposed for a previously authorized Sales Leader project?

100. Why do you manage integration?

101. Are there non-structural buyout or relocation recommendations?

102. Are the existing and future without-plan conditions reasonable and appropriate?

103. Who manages integration?

104. When is the Sales Leader project management plan created?

105. Does the selected plan protect privacy?

106. Do there need to be organizational changes?

107. Does the implementation plan have an appropriate division of responsibilities?

2.2 Scope Management Plan: Sales Leader

108. Where do scope processes fit in?

109. What work performance data will be captured?

110. What happens if scope changes?

111. What weaknesses do you have?

112. Has your organization readiness assessment been conducted?

113. Is each item clearly and completely defined?

114. Are calculations and results of analyzes essentially correct?

115. How do you plan to control Scope Creep?

116. Are Sales Leader project leaders committed to this Sales Leader project full time?

117. What if you do not have more detailed information on the report?

118. Was the scope definition used in task sequencing?

119. Have all involved Sales Leader project stakeholders and work groups committed to the Sales Leader project?

120. Are Sales Leader project team members involved in detailed estimating and scheduling?

121. Has a quality assurance plan been developed for the Sales Leader project?

122. Does the quality assurance process provide objective verification of adherence to applicable standards, procedures & requirements?

123. Process groups – where do scope management processes fit in?

124. What should you drop in order to add something new?

125. Do you keep stake holders informed?

126. What are the Quality Assurance overheads?

127. Has the business need been clearly defined?

2.3 Requirements Management Plan: Sales Leader

128. What performance metrics will be used?

129. Define the help desk model. who will take full responsibility?

130. Who will approve the requirements (and if multiple approvers, in what order)?

131. Who is responsible for monitoring and tracking the Sales Leader project requirements?

132. Who will do the reporting and to whom will reports be delivered?

133. How will requirements be managed?

134. Do you really need to write this document at all?

135. Is it new or replacing an existing business system or process?

136. In case of software development; Should you have a test for each code module?

137. Do you know which stakeholders will participate in the requirements effort?

138. What is the earliest finish date for this Sales Leader project if it is scheduled to start on ...?

139. After the requirements are gathered and set forth on the requirements register, theyre little more than a laundry list of items. Some may be duplicates, some might conflict with others and some will be too broad or too vague to understand. Describe how the requirements will be analyzed. Who will perform the analysis?

140. Should you include sub-activities?

141. How detailed should the Sales Leader project get?

142. Which hardware or software, related to, or as outcome of the Sales Leader project is new to your organization?

143. Are actual resources expenditures versus planned expenditures acceptable?

144. Is the system software (non-operating system) new to the IT Sales Leader project team?

145. What cost metrics will be used?

146. How will unresolved questions be handled once approval has been obtained?

147. Will the contractors involved take full responsibility?

2.4 Requirements Documentation: Sales Leader

148. Are there any requirements conflicts?

149. The problem with gathering requirements is right there in the word gathering. What images does it conjure?

150. Are there legal issues?

151. How do you get the user to tell you what they want?

152. Consistency. are there any requirements conflicts?

153. Are all functions required by the customer included?

154. Who is interacting with the system?

155. How will requirements be documented and who signs off on them?

156. How will they be documented / shared?

157. What is the risk associated with the technology?

158. What kind of entity is a problem ?

159. If applicable; are there issues linked with the fact that this is an offshore Sales Leader project?

160. What variations exist for a process?

161. What is your Elevator Speech?

162. Is new technology needed?

163. What are the attributes of a customer?

164. Where do you define what is a customer, what are the attributes of customer?

165. Is your business case still valid?

166. Has requirements gathering uncovered information that would necessitate changes?

2.5 Requirements Traceability Matrix: Sales Leader

167. What are the chronologies, contingencies, consequences, criteria?

168. What is the WBS?

169. What percentage of Sales Leader projects are producing traceability matrices between requirements and other work products?

170. How do you manage scope?

171. Describe the process for approving requirements so they can be added to the traceability matrix and Sales Leader project work can be performed. Will the Sales Leader project requirements become approved in writing?

172. Why use a WBS?

173. Is there a requirements traceability process in place?

174. How will it affect the stakeholders personally in career?

175. How small is small enough?

176. Why do you manage scope?

177. Do you have a clear understanding of all

subcontracts in place?

178. Will you use a Requirements Traceability Matrix?

2.6 Project Scope Statement: Sales Leader

179. Is the plan for Sales Leader project resources adequate?

180. Is there a baseline plan against which to measure progress?

181. What are the possible consequences should a risk come to occur?

182. Is the plan for your organization of the Sales Leader project resources adequate?

183. Sales Leader project lead, team lead, solution architect?

184. Will the Sales Leader project risks be managed according to the Sales Leader projects risk management process?

185. Were potential customers involved early in the planning process?

186. What is the most common tool for helping define the detail?

187. Where and how does the team fit within your organization structure?

188. Are there completion/verification criteria defined for each task producing an output?

189. Have you been able to easily identify success criteria and create objective measurements for each of the Sales Leader project scopes goal statements?

190. How will you verify the accuracy of the work of the Sales Leader project, and what constitutes acceptance of the deliverables?

191. Has everyone approved the Sales Leader projects scope statement?

192. What actions will be taken to mitigate the risk?

193. Elements that deal with providing the detail?

194. Are there adequate Sales Leader project control systems?

195. Change management vs. change leadership - what is the difference?

196. Have you been able to thoroughly document the Sales Leader projects assumptions and constraints?

197. Will statistics related to QA be collected, trends analyzed, and problems raised as issues?

2.7 Assumption and Constraint Log: Sales Leader

198. Is the amount of effort justified by the anticipated value of forming a new process?

199. Are you meeting your customers expectations consistently?

200. Have all involved stakeholders and work groups committed to the Sales Leader project?

201. Are funding and staffing resource estimates sufficiently detailed and documented for use in planning and tracking the Sales Leader project?

202. Has the approach and development strategy of the Sales Leader project been defined, documented and accepted by the appropriate stakeholders?

203. Should factors be unpredictable over time?

204. Can you perform this task or activity in a more effective manner?

205. Do documented requirements exist for all critical components and areas, including technical, business, interfaces, performance, security and conversion requirements?

206. Are there processes in place to ensure internal consistency between the source code components?

207. What would you gain if you spent time working to improve this process?

208. Does a specific action and/or state that is known to violate security policy occur?

209. Does the document/deliverable meet all requirements (for example, statement of work) specific to this deliverable?

210. What do you log?

211. What if failure during recovery?

212. When can log be discarded?

213. After observing execution of process, is it in compliance with the documented Plan?

214. Would known impacts serve as impediments?

215. What to do at recovery?

216. What do you audit?

217. Are there procedures in place to effectively manage interdependencies with other Sales Leader projects / systems?

2.8 Work Breakdown Structure: Sales Leader

218. Why is it useful?

219. How many levels?

220. When does it have to be done?

221. Where does it take place?

222. Do you need another level?

223. Can you make it?

224. When would you develop a Work Breakdown Structure?

225. How big is a work-package?

226. When do you stop?

227. What has to be done?

228. Who has to do it?

229. How will you and your Sales Leader project team define the Sales Leader projects scope and work breakdown structure?

230. How far down?

231. Why would you develop a Work Breakdown

Structure?

232. Is it still viable?

233. How much detail?

2.9 WBS Dictionary: Sales Leader

234. Are data being used by managers in an effective manner to ascertain Sales Leader project or functional status, to identify reasons or significant variance, and to initiate appropriate corrective action?

235. Does the contractors system provide unit or lot costs when applicable?

236. What went right?

237. Changes in the direct base to which overhead costs are allocated?

238. Are overhead cost budgets (or Sales Leader projections) established on a facility-wide basis at least annually for the life of the contract?

239. The wbs is developed as part of a joint planning session. and how do you know that youhave done this right?

240. Are management actions taken to reduce indirect costs when there are significant adverse variances?

241. Changes in the nature of the overhead requirements?

242. Is each control account assigned to a single organizational element directly responsible for the work and identifiable to a single element of the CWBS?

243. Are estimates of costs at completion utilized in determining contract funding requirements and reporting them?

244. Are the latest revised estimates of costs at completion compared with the established budgets at appropriate levels and causes of variances identified?

245. Are the contractors estimates of costs at completion reconcilable with cost data reported to us?

246. Are records maintained to show how management reserves are used?

247. Does the contractors system identify work accomplishment against the schedule plan?

248. Appropriate work authorization documents which subdivide the contractual effort and responsibilities, within functional organizations?

249. The total budget for the contract (including estimates for authorized and unpriced work)?

250. Is undistributed budget limited to contract effort which cannot yet be planned to CWBS elements at or below the level specified for reporting to the Government?

251. Are data elements summarized through the functional organizational structure for progressively higher levels of management?

2.10 Schedule Management Plan: Sales Leader

252. Where is the scheduling tool and who has access to it to view it?

253. Are the people assigned to the Sales Leader project sufficiently qualified?

254. Is a process for scheduling and reporting defined, including forms and formats?

255. Are estimating assumptions and constraints captured?

256. Have all unresolved risks been documented?

257. Why conduct schedule analysis?

258. Is the assigned Sales Leader project manager a PMP (Certified Sales Leader project manager) and experienced?

259. Is the correct WBS element identified for each task and milestone in the IMS?

260. Perform reality checks on schedules – are all tasks included?

261. Is there an excessive and invalid use of task constraints and relationships of leads/lags?

262. Is the steering committee active in Sales Leader

project oversight?

263. Is quality monitored from the perspective of the customers needs and expectations?

264. Are cause and effect determined for risks when they occur?

265. Are tasks tracked by hours?

266. Is your organization certified as a broker of the products/supplies?

267. Are trade-offs between accepting the risk and mitigating the risk identified?

268. Are Sales Leader project leaders committed to this Sales Leader project full time?

269. What will be the format of the schedule model?

270. Is pert / critical path or equivalent methodology being used?

271. Have Sales Leader project management standards and procedures been identified / established and documented?

2.11 Activity List: Sales Leader

272. What are you counting on?

273. Is infrastructure setup part of your Sales Leader project?

274. How do you determine the late start (LS) for each activity?

275. What is the probability the Sales Leader project can be completed in xx weeks?

276. What went wrong?

277. How detailed should a Sales Leader project get?

278. What did not go as well?

279. In what sequence?

280. What is the total time required to complete the Sales Leader project if no delays occur?

281. Who will perform the work?

282. How should ongoing costs be monitored to try to keep the Sales Leader project within budget?

283. What are the critical bottleneck activities?

284. When do the individual activities need to start and finish?

285. What went well?

286. Where will it be performed?

287. What will be performed?

288. How can the Sales Leader project be displayed graphically to better visualize the activities?

2.12 Activity Attributes: Sales Leader

289. How else could the items be grouped?

290. How many days do you need to complete the work scope with a limit of X number of resources?

291. Why?

292. How difficult will it be to complete specific activities on this Sales Leader project?

293. Were there other ways you could have organized the data to achieve similar results?

294. Activity: what is Missing?

295. What is missing?

296. Have constraints been applied to the start and finish milestones for the phases?

297. What conclusions/generalizations can you draw from this?

298. Are the required resources available or need to be acquired?

299. Is there anything planned that does not need to be here?

300. Can more resources be added?

301. Where else does it apply?

302. How much activity detail is required?

303. Have you identified the Activity Leveling Priority code value on each activity?

304. Has management defined a definite timeframe for the turnaround or Sales Leader project window?

305. What activity do you think you should spend the most time on?

306. Would you consider either of corresponding activities an outlier?

2.13 Milestone List: Sales Leader

307. Reliability of data, plan predictability?

308. Can you derive how soon can the whole Sales Leader project finish?

309. How late can the activity finish?

310. What has been done so far?

311. What are your competitors vulnerabilities?

312. Identify critical paths (one or more) and which activities are on the critical path?

313. Sustainable financial backing?

314. Which path is the critical path?

315. What specific improvements did you make to the Sales Leader project proposal since the previous time?

316. It is to be a narrative text providing the crucial aspects of your Sales Leader project proposal answering what, who, how, when and where?

317. Do you foresee any technical risks or developmental challenges?

318. How will you get the word out to customers?

319. Loss of key staff?

320. How soon can the activity finish?

321. Describe your organizations strengths and core competencies. What factors will make your organization succeed?

322. What background experience, skills, and strengths does the team bring to your organization?

323. Usps (unique selling points)?

324. How will the milestone be verified?

325. Timescales, deadlines and pressures?

326. Information and research?

2.14 Network Diagram: Sales Leader

327. Where do you schedule uncertainty time?

328. Why must you schedule milestones, such as reviews, throughout the Sales Leader project?

329. Are the required resources available?

330. If a current contract exists, can you provide the vendor name, contract start, and contract expiration date?

331. Planning: who, how long, what to do?

332. Review the logical flow of the network diagram. Take a look at which activities you have first and then sequence the activities. Do they make sense?

333. What activity must be completed immediately before this activity can start?

334. How confident can you be in your milestone dates and the delivery date?

335. What activities must follow this activity?

336. What job or jobs could run concurrently?

337. What job or jobs precede it?

338. What job or jobs follow it?

339. What activities must occur simultaneously with

this activity?

340. Are you on time?

341. What controls the start and finish of a job?

342. What can be done concurrently?

343. What to do and When?

344. What is the completion time?

345. Are the gantt chart and/or network diagram updated periodically and used to assess the overall Sales Leader project timetable?

2.15 Activity Resource Requirements: Sales Leader

346. Are there unresolved issues that need to be addressed?

347. Time for overtime?

348. When does monitoring begin?

349. Anything else?

350. Which logical relationship does the PDM use most often?

351. How do you manage time?

352. Other support in specific areas?

353. Do you use tools like decomposition and rolling-wave planning to produce the activity list and other outputs?

354. How many signatures do you require on a check and does this match what is in your policy and procedures?

355. Organizational Applicability?

356. How do you handle petty cash?

357. What are constraints that you might find during the Human Resource Planning process?

358. What is the Work Plan Standard?

359. Why do you do that?

2.16 Resource Breakdown Structure: Sales Leader

360. Which resources should be in the resource pool?

361. Who needs what information?

362. What defines a successful Sales Leader project?

363. Who delivers the information?

364. How can this help you with team building?

365. The list could probably go on, but, the thing that you would most like to know is, How long & How much?

366. Goals for the Sales Leader project. What is each stakeholders desired outcome for the Sales Leader project?

367. Who will use the system?

368. Who will be used as a Sales Leader project team member?

369. What is the number one predictor of a groups productivity?

370. What is Sales Leader project communication management?

371. What can you do to improve productivity?

372. Why do you do it?

373. Why time management?

374. When do they need the information?

375. What is the purpose of assigning and documenting responsibility?

376. What is your organizations history in doing similar activities?

2.17 Activity Duration Estimates: Sales Leader

377. What questions do you have about the sample documents provided?

378. Are activity dependencies documented?

379. Which does one need in order to complete schedule development?

380. Total slack can be calculated by which equations?

381. Which tips for taking the PMP exam do you think would be most helpful for you?

382. Are activity dependencies identified?

383. Who will provide training for the new application?

384. Are contractor costs, schedule and technical performance monitored throughout the Sales Leader project?

385. Is the work performed reviewed against contractual objectives?

386. When would a milestone chart be used instead of a bar char?

387. Are training needs identified when resources do not have the required skills to complete Sales Leader

project activities?

388. Is action taken to increase the effectiveness and efficiency of Sales Leader projects?

389. What are the largest companies that provide information technology outsourcing services?

390. Where do schedules come from?

391. Which is a benefit of an analogous Sales Leader project estimate?

392. Do procedures exist describing how the Sales Leader project scope will be managed?

393. What are some general rules of thumb for deciding if cost variance, schedule variance, cost performance index, and schedule performance index numbers are good or bad?

394. Explanation notice how many choices are half right?

395. Briefly summarize the work done by Maslow, Herzberg, McClellan, McGregor, Ouchi, Thamhain and Wilemon, and Covey. How do theories relate to Sales Leader project management?

2.18 Duration Estimating Worksheet: Sales Leader

396. Can the Sales Leader project be constructed as planned?

397. What is an Average Sales Leader project?

398. Why estimate time and cost?

399. When, then?

400. What is cost and Sales Leader project cost management?

401. For other activities, how much delay can be tolerated?

402. What is next?

403. What utility impacts are there?

404. Define the work as completely as possible. What work will be included in the Sales Leader project?

405. How should ongoing costs be monitored to try to keep the Sales Leader project within budget?

406. What questions do you have?

407. How can the Sales Leader project be displayed graphically to better visualize the activities?

408. Value pocket identification & quantification what are value pockets?

409. What is the total time required to complete the Sales Leader project if no delays occur?

410. Is the Sales Leader project responsive to community need?

411. Is a construction detail attached (to aid in explanation)?

2.19 Project Schedule: Sales Leader

412. Why do you think schedule issues often cause the most conflicts on Sales Leader projects?

413. It allows the Sales Leader project to be delivered on schedule. How Do you Use Schedules?

414. What is the difference?

415. How do you manage Sales Leader project Risk?

416. How can you minimize or control changes to Sales Leader project schedules?

417. Did the Sales Leader project come in on schedule?

418. How do you know that youhave done this right?

419. Why is software Sales Leader project disaster so common?

420. Are the original Sales Leader project schedule and budget realistic?

421. What is the most mis-scheduled part of process?

422. How does a Sales Leader project get to be a year late ?

423. Did the Sales Leader project come in under budget?

424. Are procedures defined by which the Sales Leader project schedule may be changed?

425. Meet requirements?

426. Your best shot for providing estimations how complex/how much work does the activity require?

427. How can you address that situation?

428. Activity charts and bar charts are graphical representations of a Sales Leader project schedule ...how do they differ?

2.20 Cost Management Plan: Sales Leader

429. Is an industry recognized mechanized support tool(s) being used for Sales Leader project scheduling & tracking?

430. Schedule preparation – how will the schedules be prepared during each phase of the Sales Leader project?

431. Is there a requirements change management processes in place?

432. Are metrics used to evaluate and manage Vendors?

433. Personnel with expertise?

434. Is stakeholder involvement adequate?

435. Sales Leader project Objectives?

436. Resources – how will human resources be scheduled during each phase of the Sales Leader project?

437. Is there an onboarding process in place?

438. Exclusions – is there scope to be performed or provided by others?

439. Has a sponsor been identified?

440. Cost variances – how will cost variances be identified and corrected?

441. How does the proposed individual meet each requirement?

442. Is there a formal set of procedures supporting Issues Management?

443. Are multiple estimation methods being employed?

444. Is Sales Leader project status reviewed with the steering and executive teams at appropriate intervals?

445. Does the schedule include Sales Leader project management time and change request analysis time?

446. Are Sales Leader project team members committed fulltime?

2.21 Activity Cost Estimates: Sales Leader

447. Does the estimator have experience?

448. Were the costs or charges reasonable?

449. What happens if you cannot produce the documentation for the single audit?

450. Did the Sales Leader project team have the right skills?

451. What areas does the group agree are the biggest success on the Sales Leader project?

452. Performance bond should always provide what part of the contract value?

453. Will you use any tools, such as Sales Leader project management software, to assist in capturing Earned Value metrics?

454. What communication items need improvement?

455. Is costing method consistent with study goals?

456. Review – what are some common errors in activities to avoid?

457. Certification of actual expenditures?

458. In which phase of the acquisition process cycle

does source qualifications reside?

459. Was the consultant knowledgeable about the program?

460. How do you allocate indirect costs to activities?

461. The impact and what actions were taken?

462. Can you delete activities or make them inactive?

463. Padding is bad and contingencies are good. what is the difference?

464. Were escalated issues resolved promptly?

2.22 Cost Estimating Worksheet: Sales Leader

465. Will the Sales Leader project collaborate with the local community and leverage resources?

466. What happens to any remaining funds not used?

467. What additional Sales Leader project(s) could be initiated as a result of this Sales Leader project?

468. Who is best positioned to know and assist in identifying corresponding factors?

469. Identify the timeframe necessary to monitor progress and collect data to determine how the selected measure has changed?

470. Ask: are others positioned to know, are others credible, and will others cooperate?

471. Can a trend be established from historical performance data on the selected measure and are the criteria for using trend analysis or forecasting methods met?

472. What info is needed?

473. What will others want?

474. What is the purpose of estimating?

475. How will the results be shared and to whom?

476. Does the Sales Leader project provide innovative ways for stakeholders to overcome obstacles or deliver better outcomes?

477. What costs are to be estimated?

478. Is it feasible to establish a control group arrangement?

479. What is the estimated labor cost today based upon this information?

480. What can be included?

481. Is the Sales Leader project responsive to community need?

2.23 Cost Baseline: Sales Leader

482. Escalation criteria met?

483. Vac -variance at completion, how much over/ under budget do you expect to be?

484. What is the most important thing to do next to make your Sales Leader project successful?

485. Have the resources used by the Sales Leader project been reassigned to other units or Sales Leader projects?

486. Has the Sales Leader projected annual cost to operate and maintain the product(s) or service(s) been approved and funded?

487. Have all approved changes to the Sales Leader project requirement been identified and impact on the performance, cost, and schedule baselines documented?

488. Verify business objectives. Are others appropriate, and well-articulated?

489. Are you meeting with your team regularly?

490. Have all the product or service deliverables been accepted by the customer?

491. Will the Sales Leader project fail if the change request is not executed?

492. What is the consequence?

493. What can go wrong?

494. What deliverables come first?

495. Does the suggested change request represent a desired enhancement to the products functionality?

496. For what purpose ?

497. Impact to environment?

498. Eac -estimate at completion, what is the total job expected to cost?

499. Review your risk triggers -have your risks changed?

500. Definition of done can be traced back to the definitions of what are you providing to the customer in terms of deliverables?

501. What is your organizations history in doing similar tasks?

2.24 Quality Management Plan: Sales Leader

502. If it is out of compliance, should the process be amended or should the Plan be amended?

503. How do you decide who is responsible for signing the data reports?

504. Are there trends or hot spots?

505. Are there procedures in place to effectively manage interdependencies with other Sales Leader projects / systems?

506. What is quality planning ?

507. Why quality management?

508. Who gets results of work?

509. How is staff trained?

510. How is the information recorded?

511. Can it be done better?

512. How do you prioritize?

513. How does your organization manage work to promote cooperation, individual initiative, innovation, flexibility, communications, and knowledge/skill sharing across work units?

514. How is staff trained in procedures?

515. Modifications to the requirements?

516. What are your organizations current levels and trends for the already stated measures related to customer satisfaction/ dissatisfaction and product/ service performance?

517. Is there a Quality Management Plan?

518. Have Sales Leader project management standards and procedures been established and documented?

519. Is this a Requirement?

520. Would impacts defined serve as impediments?

2.25 Quality Metrics: Sales Leader

521. What metrics do you measure?

522. What percentage are outcome-based?

523. Is a risk containment plan in place?

524. Which are the right metrics to use?

525. How should customers provide input?

526. Can visual measures help you to filter visualizations of interest?

527. Is material complete (and does it meet the standards)?

528. Is there a set of procedures to capture, analyze and act on quality metrics?

529. What about still open problems?

530. What is the CMS Benchmark?

531. How exactly do you define when differences exist?

532. What happens if you get an abnormal result?

533. Filter visualizations of interest?

534. Did the team meet the Sales Leader project success criteria documented in the Quality Metrics

Matrix?

535. What is the timeline to meet your goal?

536. Have alternatives been defined in the event that failure occurs?

537. What level of statistical confidence do you use?

538. Subjective quality component: customer satisfaction, how do you measure it?

539. Is there alignment within your organization on definitions?

540. Where is quality now?

2.26 Process Improvement Plan: Sales Leader

541. Where are you now?

542. Where do you focus?

543. Have the frequency of collection and the points in the process where measurements will be made been determined?

544. What lessons have you learned so far?

545. Where do you want to be?

546. What actions are needed to address the problems and achieve the goals?

547. How do you measure?

548. Are you making progress on the improvement framework?

549. What makes people good SPI coaches?

550. What personnel are the champions for the initiative?

551. What is the return on investment?

552. Have the supporting tools been developed or acquired?

553. Has the time line required to move measurement results from the points of collection to databases or users been established?

554. To elicit goal statements, do you ask a question such as, What do you want to achieve?

555. Are you making progress on your improvement plan?

556. Management commitment at all levels?

557. Has a process guide to collect the data been developed?

558. Why do you want to achieve the goal?

559. How do you manage quality?

560. What personnel are the sponsors for that initiative?

2.27 Responsibility Assignment Matrix: Sales Leader

561. No rs: if a task has no one listed as responsible, who is getting the job done?

562. Actual cost of work performed?

563. What are some important Sales Leader project communications management tools?

564. How many people do you need?

565. Who is going to do that work?

566. Direct labor dollars and/or hours?

567. Is work progressively subdivided into detailed work packages as requirements are defined?

568. What do you need to implement earned value management?

569. Evaluate the performance of operating organizations?

570. What expertise is available in your department?

571. With too many people labeled as doing the work, are there too many hands involved?

572. Detailed schedules which support control account and work package start and completion

dates/events?

573. Changes in the overhead pool and/or organization structures?

574. Does the accounting system provide a basis for auditing records of direct costs chargeable to the contract?

575. Do managers and team members provide helpful suggestions during review meetings?

576. Are data elements reconcilable between internal summary reports and reports forwarded to stakeholders?

577. How do you manage remotely to staff in other Divisions?

2.28 Roles and Responsibilities: Sales Leader

578. Are governance roles and responsibilities documented?

579. Key conclusions and recommendations: Are conclusions and recommendations relevant and acceptable?

580. Once the responsibilities are defined for the Sales Leader project, have the deliverables, roles and responsibilities been clearly communicated to every participant?

581. Are your policies supportive of a culture of quality data?

582. Do the values and practices inherent in the culture of your organization foster or hinder the process?

583. What should you do now to ensure that you are exceeding expectations and excelling in your current position?

584. What are your major roles and responsibilities in the area of performance measurement and assessment?

585. Who: who is involved?

586. Who is involved?

587. What expectations were met?

588. Concern: where are you limited or have no authority, where you can not influence?

589. Where are you most strong as a supervisor?

590. Attainable / achievable: the goal is attainable; can you actually accomplish the goal?

591. To decide whether to use a quality measurement, ask how will you know when it is achieved?

592. What is working well within your organizations performance management system?

593. Be specific; avoid generalities. Thank you and great work alone are insufficient. What exactly do you appreciate and why?

594. Accountabilities: what are the roles and responsibilities of individual team members?

595. Required skills, knowledge, experience?

596. What is working well?

597. Are Sales Leader project team roles and responsibilities identified and documented?

2.29 Human Resource Management Plan: Sales Leader

598. What areas does the group agree are the biggest success on the Sales Leader project?

599. Are internal Sales Leader project status meetings held at reasonable intervals?

600. What talent is needed?

601. Are risk triggers captured?

602. Is your organization heading towards expansion, outsourcing of certain talents or making cut-backs to save money?

603. Is a stakeholder management plan in place that covers topics?

604. Does a documented Sales Leader project organizational policy & plan (i.e. governance model) exist?

605. Are vendor invoices audited for accuracy before payment?

606. Is it possible to track all classes of Sales Leader project work (e.g. scheduled, un-scheduled, defect repair, etc.)?

607. Has a quality assurance plan been developed for the Sales Leader project?

608. Are staff skills known and available for each task?

609. Is a payment system in place with proper reviews and approvals?

610. Are changes in deliverable commitments agreed to by all affected groups & individuals?

611. Is there an issues management plan in place?

612. Are software metrics formally captured, analyzed and used as a basis for other Sales Leader project estimates?

613. Has a capability assessment been conducted?

2.30 Communications Management Plan: Sales Leader

614. Will messages be directly related to the release strategy or phases of the Sales Leader project?

615. What communications method?

616. Do you then often overlook a key stakeholder or stakeholder group?

617. Are there common objectives between the team and the stakeholder?

618. Which stakeholders are thought leaders, influences, or early adopters?

619. Who is the stakeholder?

620. Who have you worked with in past, similar initiatives?

621. Are stakeholders internal or external?

622. What is Sales Leader project communications management?

623. Are the stakeholders getting the information others need, are others consulted, are concerns addressed?

624. Who were proponents/opponents?

625. How is this initiative related to other portfolios, programs, or Sales Leader projects?

626. Who will use or be affected by the result of a Sales Leader project?

627. Why is stakeholder engagement important?

628. In your work, how much time is spent on stakeholder identification?

629. Are there too many who have an interest in some aspect of your work?

630. What does the stakeholder need from the team?

631. Are you constantly rushing from meeting to meeting?

632. What approaches to you feel are the best ones to use?

633. Why do you manage communications?

2.31 Risk Management Plan: Sales Leader

634. People risk -are people with appropriate skills available to help complete the Sales Leader project?

635. User involvement: do you have the right users?

636. How would you suggest monitoring for risk transition indicators?

637. Which risks should get the attention?

638. What things might go wrong?

639. Are flexibility and reuse paramount?

640. Can the Sales Leader project proceed without assuming the risk?

641. Who should be notified of the occurrence of each of the indicators?

642. How is risk identification performed?

643. What can you do to minimize the impact if it does?

644. Do you have a consistent repeatable process that is actually used?

645. What is the probability the risk avoidance strategy will be successful?

646. Does the Sales Leader project have the authority and ability to avoid the risk?

647. Financial risk -can your organization afford to undertake the Sales Leader project?

648. What are some questions that should be addressed in a risk management plan?

649. Have staff received necessary training?

650. Management -what contingency plans do you have if the risk becomes a reality?

651. What will the damage be?

652. What does a risk management program do?

653. Market risk -will the new service or product be useful to your organization or marketable to others?

2.32 Risk Register: Sales Leader

654. Who needs to know about this?

655. Having taken action, how did the responses effect change, and where is the Sales Leader project now?

656. What will be done?

657. What should you do when?

658. Who is going to do it?

659. Is further information required before making a decision?

660. Why would you develop a risk register?

661. What is the appropriate level of risk management for this Sales Leader project?

662. What are the main aims, objectives of the policy, strategy, or service and the intended outcomes?

663. Are there any gaps in the evidence?

664. People risk -are people with appropriate skills available to help complete the Sales Leader project?

665. Financial risk -can your organization afford to undertake the Sales Leader project?

666. What further options might be available for

responding to the risk?

667. When will it happen?

668. How are risks identified?

669. What is a Risk?

670. Schedule impact/severity estimated range (workdays) assume the event happens, what is the potential impact?

671. What action, if any, has been taken to respond to the risk?

2.33 Probability and Impact Assessment: Sales Leader

672. What is the risk appetite?

673. Does the customer understand the software process?

674. Why has this particular mode of contracting been chosen?

675. What are the chances the risk event will occur?

676. What should be done with non-critical risks?

677. How do you maximize short-term return on investment?

678. What is the probability of the risk occurring?

679. Have you ascribed a level of confidence to every critical technical objective?

680. Can it be enlarged by drawing people from other areas of your organization?

681. Do you train all developers in the process?

682. Is the customer technically sophisticated in the product area?

683. Are trained personnel, including supervisors and Sales Leader project managers, available to handle

such a large Sales Leader project?

684. Your customers business requirements have suddenly shifted because of a new regulatory statute, what now?

685. Can the Sales Leader project proceed without assuming the risk?

686. What risks does the employee encounter?

687. Risk data quality assessment - what is the quality of the data used to determine or assess the risk?

688. Has the need for the Sales Leader project been properly established?

689. Is the present organizational structure for handling the Sales Leader project sufficient?

690. Which functions, departments, and activities of your organization are going to be affected?

691. Who are the international/overseas Sales Leader project partners (equipment supplier/supplier/consultant/contractor) for this Sales Leader project?

2.34 Probability and Impact Matrix: Sales Leader

692. Lay ground work for future returns?

693. Economic to take on the Sales Leader project?

694. Sensitivity analysis -which risks will have the most impact on the Sales Leader project?

695. Several experts are offsite, and wish to be included. How can this be done?

696. Which of your Sales Leader projects should be selected when compared with other Sales Leader projects?

697. What are the risks involved in appointing external agencies to manage the Sales Leader project?

698. Who has experience with this?

699. Are you working on the right risks?

700. What are the uncertainties associated with the technology selected for the Sales Leader project?

701. What are the probable external agencies to act as Sales Leader project manager?

702. Are Sales Leader project requirements stable?

703. Has the need for the Sales Leader project been

properly established?

704. Who is going to be the consortium leader?

705. What do you expect?

706. The customer requests a change to the Sales Leader project that would increase the Sales Leader project risk. Which should you do before ass the others?

707. What changes in the regulation are forthcoming?

708. Do you have a mechanism for managing change?

709. Are the risk data complete?

2.35 Risk Data Sheet: Sales Leader

710. What are your core values?

711. What can you do?

712. What if client refuses?

713. Has the most cost-effective solution been chosen?

714. Potential for recurrence?

715. What will be the consequences if the risk happens?

716. Type of risk identified?

717. What are the main opportunities available to you that you should grab while you can?

718. What are the main threats to your existence?

719. What is the environment within which you operate (social trends, economic, community values, broad based participation, national directions etc.)?

720. What were the Causes that contributed?

721. If it happens, what are the consequences?

722. How reliable is the data source?

723. What will be the consequences if it happens?

724. What is the likelihood of it happening?

725. What do people affected think about the need for, and practicality of preventive measures?

726. What are you here for (Mission)?

727. What are you trying to achieve (Objectives)?

728. What are you weak at and therefore need to do better?

2.36 Procurement Management Plan: Sales Leader

729. Are the payment terms being followed?

730. Has a provision been made to reassess Sales Leader project risks at various Sales Leader project stages?

731. Are stakeholders aware and supportive of the principles and practices of modern software estimation?

732. Is there a formal process for updating the Sales Leader project baseline?

733. Has a structured approach been used to break work effort into manageable components (WBS)?

734. Are the Sales Leader project plans updated on a frequent basis?

735. Do Sales Leader project teams & team members report on status / activities / progress?

736. Are Sales Leader project leaders committed to this Sales Leader project full time?

737. How and when do you enter into Sales Leader project Procurement Management?

738. Was your organizations estimating methodology being used and followed?

739. Is it possible to track all classes of Sales Leader project work (e.g. scheduled, un-scheduled, defect repair, etc.)?

740. What are things that you need to improve?

741. Have process improvement efforts been completed before requirements efforts begin?

742. Does the schedule include Sales Leader project management time and change request analysis time?

743. Was an original risk assessment/risk management plan completed?

744. Has the Sales Leader project manager been identified?

745. Does the business case include how the Sales Leader project aligns with your organizations strategic goals & objectives?

2.37 Source Selection Criteria: Sales Leader

746. Are they compliant with all technical requirements?

747. Does your documentation identify why the team concurs or differs with reported performance from past performance report (CPARs, questionnaire responses, etc.)?

748. What information may not be provided?

749. Team leads: what is your process for assigning ratings?

750. When must you conduct a debriefing?

751. How are clarifications and communications appropriately used?

752. What does a sample rating scale look like?

753. Does an evaluation need to include the identification of strengths and weaknesses?

754. What are open book debriefings?

755. When is it appropriate to conduct a preproposal conference?

756. Is the contracting office likely to receive more purchase requests for this item or service during the

coming year?

757. How important is cost in the source selection decision relative to past performance and technical considerations?

758. In the technical/management area, what criteria do you use to determine the final evaluation ratings?

759. What past performance information should be requested?

760. Is a cost realism analysis used?

761. How should the preproposal conference be conducted?

762. How do you consolidate reviews and analysis of evaluators?

763. What common questions or problems are associated with debriefings?

764. What risks were identified in the proposals?

765. How long will it take for the purchase cost to be the same as the lease cost?

2.38 Stakeholder Management Plan: Sales Leader

766. Are corrective actions and variances reported?

767. Pareto diagrams, statistical sampling, flow charting or trend analysis used quality monitoring?

768. When would you develop a Sales Leader project Business Plan?

769. Are the schedule estimates reasonable given the Sales Leader project?

770. If a problem has been detected, what tools can be used to determine a root cause?

771. Are changes in scope (deliverable commitments) agreed to by all affected groups & individuals?

772. In your opinion, do certain Sales Leader project resources hold a higher importance than other resources?

773. Are decisions captured in a decisions log?

774. What proven methodologies and standards will be used to ensure that materials, products, processes and services are fit for purpose?

775. Is the assigned Sales Leader project manager a PMP (Certified Sales Leader project manager) and experienced?

776. Has a Sales Leader project Communications Plan been developed?

777. Are there unnecessary steps that are creating bottlenecks and/or causing people to wait?

778. Do you know what your customers expectations are regarding this process?

779. Are all resource assumptions documented?

780. Are all vendor contracts closed out?

781. Who is responsible for arranging and managing the review(s)?

782. Are mitigation strategies identified?

783. What other teams / processes would be impacted by changes to the current process, and how?

784. Have the key elements of a coherent Sales Leader project management strategy been established?

2.39 Change Management Plan: Sales Leader

785. What are the key change management success metrics?

786. What risks may occur upfront, during implementation and after implementation?

787. What are the current methods of sharing information and do there need to be new ones developed?

788. Has the training co-ordinator been provided with the training details and put in place the necessary arrangements?

789. Will a different work structure focus people on what is important?

790. How frequently should you repeat the message?

791. Has this been negotiated with the customer and sponsor?

792. What is the worst thing that can happen if you chose not to communicate this information?

793. What new roles are needed?

794. Who might be able to help you the most?

795. What are the training strategies?

796. Who might present the most resistance?

797. What relationships will change?

798. Who will be the change levers?

799. Has the target training audience been identified and nominated?

800. How might they respond to the message and if the response may be negative or open to misinterpretation, what else needs to be said?

801. What are you trying to achieve as a result of communication?

802. Has the training provider been established?

3.0 Executing Process Group: Sales Leader

803. Is the program supported by national and/or local organizations?

804. What type of people would you want on your team?

805. What is involved in the solicitation process?

806. What are the challenges Sales Leader project teams face?

807. Is activity definition the first process involved in Sales Leader project time management?

808. It under budget or over budget?

809. What is the critical path for this Sales Leader project and how long is it?

810. Will a new application be developed using existing hardware, software, and networks?

811. What does it mean to take a systems view of a Sales Leader project?

812. How well did the team follow the chosen processes?

813. Will outside resources be needed to help?

814. Will additional funds be needed for hardware or software?

815. What were things that you did very well and want to do the same again on the next Sales Leader project?

816. What are the main types of goods and services being outsourced?

817. What is the difference between conceptual, application, and evaluative questions?

818. What is in place for ensuring adequate change control on Sales Leader projects that involve outside contracts?

819. Do Sales Leader project managers understand your organizational context for Sales Leader projects?

820. What good practices or successful experiences or transferable examples have been identified?

821. What type of information goes in the quality assurance plan?

822. If action is called for, what form should it take?

3.1 Team Member Status Report: Sales Leader

823. Will the staff do training or is that done by a third party?

824. Is there evidence that staff is taking a more professional approach toward management of your organizations Sales Leader projects?

825. What is to be done?

826. When a teams productivity and success depend on collaboration and the efficient flow of information, what generally fails them?

827. Do you have an Enterprise Sales Leader project Management Office (EPMO)?

828. How much risk is involved?

829. How will resource planning be done?

830. How does this product, good, or service meet the needs of the Sales Leader project and your organization as a whole?

831. Why is it to be done?

832. Does every department have to have a Sales Leader project Manager on staff?

833. What specific interest groups do you have in

place?

834. Are the products of your organizations Sales Leader projects meeting customers objectives?

835. How it is to be done?

836. The problem with Reward & Recognition Programs is that the truly deserving people all too often get left out. How can you make it practical?

837. Does the product, good, or service already exist within your organization?

838. Are your organizations Sales Leader projects more successful over time?

839. How can you make it practical?

840. Are the attitudes of staff regarding Sales Leader project work improving?

841. Does your organization have the means (staff, money, contract, etc.) to produce or to acquire the product, good, or service?

3.2 Change Request: Sales Leader

842. Have scm procedures for noting the change, recording it, and reporting it been followed?

843. What must be taken into consideration when introducing change control programs?

844. Who needs to approve change requests?

845. What are the requirements for urgent changes?

846. Why control change across the life cycle?

847. How fast will change requests be approved?

848. What is the change request log?

849. Does the schedule include Sales Leader project management time and change request analysis time?

850. Who can suggest changes?

851. How many times must the change be modified or presented to the change control board before it is approved?

852. Can you answer what happened, who did it, when did it happen, and what else will be affected?

853. Who will perform the change?

854. How do you get changes (code) out in a timely manner?

855. What is the purpose of change control?

856. Have all related configuration items been properly updated?

857. How are changes requested (forms, method of communication)?

858. Why do you want to have a change control system?

859. Which requirements attributes affect the risk to reliability the most?

860. Who is responsible for the implementation and monitoring of all measures?

861. Since there are no change requests in your Sales Leader project at this point, what must you have before you begin?

3.3 Change Log: Sales Leader

862. Is the change backward compatible without limitations?

863. Is the change request within Sales Leader project scope?

864. Do the described changes impact on the integrity or security of the system?

865. How does this change affect the timeline of the schedule?

866. When was the request submitted?

867. Is the requested change request a result of changes in other Sales Leader project(s)?

868. Does the suggested change request seem to represent a necessary enhancement to the product?

869. Should a more thorough impact analysis be conducted?

870. When was the request approved?

871. Is the submitted change a new change or a modification of a previously approved change?

872. How does this relate to the standards developed for specific business processes?

873. Is this a mandatory replacement?

874. How does this change affect scope?

875. Will the Sales Leader project fail if the change request is not executed?

876. Is the change request open, closed or pending?

877. Who initiated the change request?

878. Where do changes come from?

3.4 Decision Log: Sales Leader

879. How does an increasing emphasis on cost containment influence the strategies and tactics used?

880. What is the average size of your matters in an applicable measurement?

881. It becomes critical to track and periodically revisit both operational effectiveness; Are you noticing all that you need to, and are you interpreting what you see effectively?

882. How do you define success?

883. Which variables make a critical difference?

884. What is the line where eDiscovery ends and document review begins?

885. Does anything need to be adjusted?

886. What eDiscovery problem or issue did your organization set out to fix or make better?

887. Linked to original objective?

888. How do you know when you are achieving it?

889. What was the rationale for the decision?

890. Who is the decisionmaker?

891. How does provision of information, both in terms of content and presentation, influence acceptance of alternative strategies?

892. With whom was the decision shared or considered?

893. What are the cost implications?

894. Decision-making process; how will the team make decisions?

895. Behaviors; what are guidelines that the team has identified that will assist them with getting the most out of team meetings?

896. What alternatives/risks were considered?

897. Do strategies and tactics aimed at less than full control reduce the costs of management or simply shift the cost burden?

898. What is your overall strategy for quality control / quality assurance procedures?

3.5 Quality Audit: Sales Leader

899. How does your organization know that its systems for providing high quality consultancy services to external parties are appropriately effective and constructive?

900. Is there a written corporate quality policy?

901. How does your organization know that its quality of teaching is appropriately effective and constructive?

902. What review processes are in place for your organizations major activities?

903. Are there appropriate means for intervening if necessary?

904. How does your organization know that its system for recruiting the best staff possible are appropriately effective and constructive?

905. How does your organization know that its system for attending to the particular needs of its international staff is appropriately effective and constructive?

906. How does your organization know that its system for staff performance planning and review is appropriately effective and constructive?

907. Do all staff have the necessary authority and resources to deliver what is expected of them?

908. How does your organization know that its processes for managing severance are appropriately effective, constructive and fair?

909. What has changed/improved as a result of the review processes?

910. Is your organizational structure a help or a hindrance to deployment?

911. How does your organization know that its management system is appropriately effective and constructive?

912. Is progress against the intentions measurable?

913. How does your organization know that its system for commercializing research outputs is appropriately effective and constructive?

914. Has a written procedure been established to identify devices during all stages of receipt, reconditioning, distribution and installation so that mix-ups are prevented?

915. Are all records associated with the reconditioning of a device maintained for a minimum of two years after the sale or disposal of the last device within a lot of merchandise?

916. How do you know what, specifically, is required of you in your work?

917. How does your organization know that its staff placements are appropriately effective and

constructive in relation to program-related learning outcomes?

918. How does your organization know that its public relations and marketing systems are appropriately effective and constructive?

3.6 Team Directory: Sales Leader

919. Process decisions: are there any statutory or regulatory issues relevant to the timely execution of work?

920. Process decisions: do job conditions warrant additional actions to collect job information and document on-site activity?

921. Is construction on schedule?

922. Decisions: is the most suitable form of contract being used?

923. Contract requirements complied with?

924. Who will write the meeting minutes and distribute?

925. Process decisions: which organizational elements and which individuals will be assigned management functions?

926. When will you produce deliverables?

927. Process decisions: are all start-up, turn over and close out requirements of the contract satisfied?

928. How does the team resolve conflicts and ensure tasks are completed?

929. Have you decided when to celebrate the Sales Leader projects completion date?

930. Why is the work necessary?

931. Who are the Team Members?

932. Who are your stakeholders (customers, sponsors, end users, team members)?

933. How and in what format should information be presented?

934. Days from the time the issue is identified?

935. How will the team handle changes?

936. Process decisions: are contractors adequately prosecuting the work?

937. Process decisions: is work progressing on schedule and per contract requirements?

3.7 Team Operating Agreement: Sales Leader

938. How does teaming fit in with overall organizational goals and meet organizational needs?

939. Did you prepare participants for the next meeting?

940. Do you post meeting notes and the recording (if used) and notify participants?

941. Do you brief absent members after they view meeting notes or listen to a recording?

942. Are team roles clearly defined and accepted?

943. How will you divide work equitably?

944. What resources can be provided for the team in terms of equipment, space, time for training, protected time and space for meetings, and travel allowances?

945. How will your group handle planned absences?

946. Do you determine the meeting length and time of day?

947. Are there more than two functional areas represented by your team?

948. What is a Virtual Team?

949. How do you want to be thought of and known within your organization?

950. Do you begin with a question to engage everyone?

951. What are the boundaries (organizational or geographic) within which you operate?

952. What are the current caseload numbers in the unit?

953. Conflict resolution: how will disputes and other conflicts be mediated or resolved?

954. What is group supervision?

955. Do you upload presentation materials in advance and test the technology?

956. Reimbursements: how will the team members be reimbursed for expenses and time commitments?

3.8 Team Performance Assessment: Sales Leader

957. When does the medium matter?

958. Do you promptly inform members about major developments that may affect them?

959. What structural changes have you made or are you preparing to make?

960. If you are worried about method variance before you collect data, what sort of design elements might you include to reduce or eliminate the threat of method variance?

961. To what degree is the team cognizant of small wins to be celebrated along the way?

962. To what degree can the team ensure that all members are individually and jointly accountable for the teams purpose, goals, approach, and work-products?

963. When a reviewer complains about method variance, what is the essence of the complaint?

964. To what degree can the team measure progress against specific goals?

965. To what degree does the team possess adequate membership to achieve its ends?

966. What are teams?

967. How do you keep key people outside the group informed about its accomplishments?

968. To what degree do team members articulate the teams work approach?

969. To what degree does the teams purpose constitute a broader, deeper aspiration than just accomplishing short-term goals?

970. Effects of crew composition on crew performance: Does the whole equal the sum of its parts?

971. What do you think is the most constructive thing that could be done now to resolve considerations and disputes about method variance?

972. To what degree are the goals realistic?

973. To what degree are the relative importance and priority of the goals clear to all team members?

974. Does more radicalness mean more perceived benefits?

975. Is there a particular method of data analysis that you would recommend as a means of demonstrating that method variance is not of great concern for a given dataset?

976. To what degree can team members meet frequently enough to accomplish the teams ends?

3.9 Team Member Performance Assessment: Sales Leader

977. Does adaptive training work?

978. Who receives a benchmark visit?

979. What tools are available to determine whether all contract functional and compliance areas of performance objectives, measures, and incentives have been met?

980. What is collaboration?

981. What are best practices for delivering and developing training evaluations to maximize the benefits of leveraging emerging technologies?

982. Are any governance changes sufficient to impact achievement?

983. How was the determination made for which training platforms would be used (i.e., media selection)?

984. How accurately is your plan implemented?

985. What stakeholders must be involved in the development and oversight of the performance plan?

986. Does the rater (supervisor) have the authority or responsibility to tell an employee that the employees performance is unsatisfactory?

987. Does statute or regulation require the job responsibility?

988. What innovations (if any) are developed to realize goals?

989. Goals met?

990. Should a ratee get a copy of all the raters documents about the employees performance?

991. To what degree does the teams purpose contain themes that are particularly meaningful and memorable?

992. What is used as a basis for instructional decisions?

993. To what degree does the teams approach to its work allow for modification and improvement over time?

994. How do you determine which data are the most important to use, analyze, or review?

995. To what degree do team members frequently explore the teams purpose and its implications?

996. How are performance measures and associated incentives developed?

3.10 Issue Log: Sales Leader

997. Are the stakeholders getting the information they need, are they consulted, are concerns addressed?

998. What would have to change?

999. Is access to the Issue Log controlled?

1000. Which team member will work with each stakeholder?

1001. What is the impact on the risks?

1002. What effort will a change need?

1003. Are the Sales Leader project issues uniquely identified, including to which product they refer?

1004. Which stakeholders can influence others?

1005. How is this initiative related to other portfolios, programs, or Sales Leader projects?

1006. What are the typical contents?

1007. How do you manage communications?

1008. What is the stakeholders level of authority?

1009. How do you reply to this question; you am new here and managing this major program. How do you suggest you build your network?

1010. Are there potential barriers between the team and the stakeholder?

1011. How often do you engage with stakeholders?

1012. Who reported the issue?

1013. Do you often overlook a key stakeholder or stakeholder group?

4.0 Monitoring and Controlling Process Group: Sales Leader

1014. How is Agile Sales Leader project Management done?

1015. Overall, how does the program function to serve the clients?

1016. How many more potential communications channels were introduced by the discovery of the new stakeholders?

1017. What resources are necessary?

1018. Is there undesirable impact on staff or resources?

1019. Were sponsors and decision makers available when needed outside regularly scheduled meetings?

1020. What business situation is being addressed?

1021. Do the partners have sufficient financial capacity to keep up the benefits produced by the programme?

1022. How well defined and documented were the Sales Leader project management processes you chose to use?

1023. If a risk event occurs, what will you do?

1024. Change, where should you look for problems?

1025. How is agile portfolio management done?

1026. How were collaborations developed, and how are they sustained?

1027. Feasibility: how much money, time, and effort can you put into this?

1028. What were things that you did well, and could improve, and how?

1029. How can you monitor progress?

1030. Did the Sales Leader project team have enough people to execute the Sales Leader project plan?

1031. Just how important is your work to the overall success of the Sales Leader project?

1032. Where is the Risk in the Sales Leader project?

4.1 Project Performance Report: Sales Leader

1033. To what degree do team members agree with the goals, relative importance, and the ways in which achievement will be measured?

1034. To what degree can team members vigorously define the teams purpose in considerations with others who are not part of the functioning team?

1035. To what degree are the teams goals and objectives clear, simple, and measurable?

1036. To what degree will the team adopt a concrete, clearly understood, and agreed-upon approach that will result in achievement of the teams goals?

1037. Next Steps?

1038. To what degree will the team ensure that all members equitably share the work essential to the success of the team?

1039. To what degree can the cognitive capacity of individuals accommodate the flow of information?

1040. To what degree are the members clear on what they are individually responsible for and what they are jointly responsible for?

1041. To what degree can all members engage in open and interactive considerations?

1042. To what degree are the tasks requirements reflected in the flow and storage of information?

1043. How can Sales Leader project sustainability be maintained?

1044. To what degree do members articulate the goals beyond the team membership?

1045. To what degree does the teams work approach provide opportunity for members to engage in results-based evaluation?

1046. To what degree does the funding match the requirement?

1047. To what degree do the relationships of the informal organization motivate taskrelevant behavior and facilitate task completion?

1048. To what degree do the structures of the formal organization motivate taskrelevant behavior and facilitate task completion?

4.2 Variance Analysis: Sales Leader

1049. What is the budgeted cost for work scheduled?

1050. Are indirect costs charged to the appropriate indirect pools and incurring organization?

1051. Did a new competitor enter the market?

1052. Why are standard cost systems used?

1053. Wbs elements contractually specified for reporting of status to your organization (lowest level only)?

1054. Is budgeted cost for work performed calculated in a manner consistent with the way work is planned?

1055. Is there a logical explanation for any variance?

1056. How do you verify authorization to proceed with all authorized work?

1057. There are detailed schedules which support control account and work package start and completion dates/events?

1058. Why do variances exist?

1059. Are authorized changes being incorporated in a timely manner?

1060. Are the actual costs used for variance analysis reconcilable with data from the accounting system?

1061. How are material, labor, and overhead standards set?

1062. What is the performance to date and material commitment?

1063. How do you identify potential or actual overruns and underruns?

1064. What does an unfavorable overhead volume variance mean?

1065. Favorable or unfavorable variance?

1066. Are the bases and rates for allocating costs from each indirect pool consistently applied?

1067. Do the rates and prices remain constant throughout the year?

1068. How does the monthly budget compare to the actual experience?

4.3 Earned Value Status: Sales Leader

1069. What is the unit of forecast value?

1070. Where are your problem areas?

1071. Where is evidence-based earned value in your organization reported?

1072. How much is it going to cost by the finish?

1073. Validation is a process of ensuring that the developed system will actually achieve the stakeholders desired outcomes; Are you building the right product? What do you validate?

1074. Earned value can be used in almost any Sales Leader project situation and in almost any Sales Leader project environment. it may be used on large Sales Leader projects, medium sized Sales Leader projects, tiny Sales Leader projects (in cut-down form), complex and simple Sales Leader projects and in any market sector. some people, of course, know all about earned value, they have used it for years - but perhaps not as effectively as they could have?

1075. If earned value management (EVM) is so good in determining the true status of a Sales Leader project and Sales Leader project its completion, why is it that hardly any one uses it in information systems related Sales Leader projects?

1076. Verification is a process of ensuring that the developed system satisfies the stakeholders agreements and specifications; Are you building the product right? What do you verify?

1077. How does this compare with other Sales Leader projects?

1078. Are you hitting your Sales Leader projects targets?

1079. When is it going to finish?

4.4 Risk Audit: Sales Leader

1080. Does your auditor understand your business?

1081. What are the boundaries of the auditors responsibility for policing management fidelity?

1082. Is there a screening process that will ensure all participants have the fitness and skills required to safely participate?

1083. What programmatic and Fiscal information is being collected and analyzed?

1084. Do requirements demand the use of new analysis, design, or testing methods?

1085. When your organization is entering into a major contract, does it seek legal advice?

1086. How effective are your risk controls?

1087. Are the best people available?

1088. If applicable; does the software interface with new or unproven hardware or unproven vendor products?

1089. What compliance systems do you have in place to address quality, errors, and outcomes?

1090. To what extent should analytical procedures be utilized in the risk-assessment process?

1091. Auditor independence: a burdensome constraint or a core value?

1092. Is safety information provided to all involved?

1093. What are the legal implications of not identifying a complete universe of business risks?

1094. What is the anticipated volatility of the requirements?

1095. What are the strategic implications with clients when auditors focus audit resources based on business-level risks?

1096. Number of users of the product?

1097. Improving fraud detection: do auditors react to abnormal inconsistencies between financial and non-financial measures?

1098. Are end-users enthusiastically committed to the Sales Leader project and the system/product to be built?

4.5 Contractor Status Report: Sales Leader

1099. How is risk transferred?

1100. What are the minimum and optimal bandwidth requirements for the proposed solution?

1101. What was the final actual cost?

1102. If applicable; describe your standard schedule for new software version releases. Are new software version releases included in the standard maintenance plan?

1103. What is the average response time for answering a support call?

1104. Who can list a Sales Leader project as organization experience, your organization or a previous employee of your organization?

1105. What was the budget or estimated cost for your organizations services?

1106. Describe how often regular updates are made to the proposed solution. Are corresponding regular updates included in the standard maintenance plan?

1107. How long have you been using the services?

1108. What was the actual budget or estimated cost for your organizations services?

1109. Are there contractual transfer concerns?

1110. What was the overall budget or estimated cost?

1111. What process manages the contracts?

4.6 Formal Acceptance: Sales Leader

1112. Was the Sales Leader project goal achieved?

1113. Was business value realized?

1114. What function(s) does it fill or meet?

1115. Do you perform formal acceptance or burn-in tests?

1116. What lessons were learned about your Sales Leader project management methodology?

1117. What is the Acceptance Management Process?

1118. What was done right?

1119. Have all comments been addressed?

1120. General estimate of the costs and times to complete the Sales Leader project?

1121. Did the Sales Leader project manager and team act in a professional and ethical manner?

1122. Was the Sales Leader project managed well?

1123. How does your team plan to obtain formal acceptance on your Sales Leader project?

1124. Do you buy-in installation services?

1125. What can you do better next time?

1126. What features, practices, and processes proved to be strengths or weaknesses?

1127. Do you buy pre-configured systems or build your own configuration?

1128. Does it do what client said it would?

1129. Who supplies data?

1130. Was the Sales Leader project work done on time, within budget, and according to specification?

1131. How well did the team follow the methodology?

5.0 Closing Process Group: Sales Leader

1132. What can you do better next time, and what specific actions can you take to improve?

1133. What could be done to improve the process?

1134. What is the Sales Leader project name and date of completion?

1135. Did the Sales Leader project team have enough people to execute the Sales Leader project plan?

1136. Was the user/client satisfied with the end product?

1137. Did the Sales Leader project management methodology work?

1138. Will the Sales Leader project deliverable(s) replace a current asset or group of assets?

1139. Does the close educate others to improve performance?

1140. What could have been improved?

1141. What is an Encumbrance?

1142. How well did the chosen processes fit the needs of the Sales Leader project?

1143. Did you do what you said you were going to do?

1144. What level of risk does the proposed budget represent to the Sales Leader project?

1145. Is this an updated Sales Leader project Proposal Document?

1146. Were cost budgets met?

1147. Did the delivered product meet the specified requirements and goals of the Sales Leader project?

5.1 Procurement Audit: Sales Leader

1148. Are buyers rotated so that they do not deal with the same vendors year in and year out?

1149. Do buyers obtain price quotations or bids from two or more suppliers on significant purchases if catalog or advertised prices are not available?

1150. Are there systems for recording and monitoring in order to discover malpractice and fraud in the procurement function/unit?

1151. Is your organization aware and informed about international procurement standards and good practice?

1152. Were bids properly evaluated?

1153. Is it on a regular basis examined whether it is possible to enter into public private partnerships with private suppliers?

1154. Are the users needs clearly and invariably defined and has the expected outcome or mission been clearly identified and communicated in measurable terms?

1155. Is procurement execution duly monitored and documented?

1156. Are advance payments to employees properly authorized and controlled?

1157. Does your organization have a purchasing policy ?

1158. How do you confirm whether the contracted organization supplied the goods or executed the work as per the quality, quantity and price indicated in the contract agreement/ supply order?

1159. Was suitability of candidates accurately assessed?

1160. Were there no material changes in the contract shortly after award?

1161. Were the tender documents comprehensive, transparent and non-discriminating?

1162. Has an upper limit of cost been fixed?

1163. Is there no evidence of favouritism towards a particular contractor during the evaluation and negotiation processes?

1164. Who are the key suppliers?

1165. Are employees with cash disbursement responsibilities required to take scheduled vacations?

1166. When you set social or environmental conditions for the performance of the contract, were corresponding compatible with the law and was adequate information given to the candidates?

1167. Are the purchase order forms designed for efficient and simple completion?

5.2 Contract Close-Out: Sales Leader

1168. Have all contract records been included in the Sales Leader project archives?

1169. What happens to the recipient of services?

1170. What is capture management?

1171. How is the contracting office notified of the automatic contract close-out?

1172. Have all contracts been completed?

1173. Was the contract sufficiently clear so as not to result in numerous disputes and misunderstandings?

1174. How does it work?

1175. Why Outsource?

1176. Have all contracts been closed?

1177. How/when used ?

1178. Was the contract complete without requiring numerous changes and revisions?

1179. Change in knowledge?

1180. Are the signers the authorized officials?

1181. Was the contract type appropriate?

1182. Parties: Authorized?

1183. Change in attitude or behavior?

1184. Has each contract been audited to verify acceptance and delivery?

1185. Parties: who is involved?

1186. Change in circumstances?

1187. Have all acceptance criteria been met prior to final payment to contractors?

5.3 Project or Phase Close-Out: Sales Leader

1188. What information did each stakeholder need to contribute to the Sales Leader projects success?

1189. What were the actual outcomes?

1190. What stakeholder group needs, expectations, and interests are being met by the Sales Leader project?

1191. Is there a clear cause and effect between the activity and the lesson learned?

1192. Did the delivered product meet the specified requirements and goals of the Sales Leader project?

1193. What advantages do the an individual interview have over a group meeting, and vice-versa?

1194. Can the lesson learned be replicated?

1195. What benefits or impacts does the stakeholder group expect to obtain as a result of the Sales Leader project?

1196. When and how were information needs best met?

1197. What hierarchical authority does the stakeholder have in your organization?

1198. What are the mandatory communication needs for each stakeholder?

1199. Who controlled the resources for the Sales Leader project?

1200. What are they?

1201. In preparing the Lessons Learned report, should it reflect a consensus viewpoint, or should the report reflect the different individual viewpoints?

1202. Which changes might a stakeholder be required to make as a result of the Sales Leader project?

1203. What is in it for you?

1204. Were risks identified and mitigated?

5.4 Lessons Learned: Sales Leader

1205. What would you approach differently next time?

1206. How much time is required for the task?

1207. To what extent was the evolution of risks communicated?

1208. For the next Sales Leader project, how could you improve on the way Sales Leader project was conducted?

1209. What were the major enablers to a quick response?

1210. How satisfied are you with your involvement in the development and/or review of the Sales Leader project Scope during Sales Leader project Initiation and Planning?

1211. What is in the future?

1212. How does the budget cycle affect the case?

1213. What is the value of the deliverable?

1214. What is the frequency of personal communications?

1215. What is the proportion of in-house and contractor personnel authorized for the Sales Leader project?

1216. How effectively and timely was your organizational change impact identified and planned for?

1217. What mistakes did you successfully avoid making?

1218. What regulatory constraints impact the case?

1219. What was the single greatest success and the single greatest shortcoming or challenge from the Sales Leader projects perspective?

1220. Was the purpose of the Sales Leader project, the end products and success criteria clearly defined and agreed at the start?

1221. What report generation capability is needed?

1222. What are the skills directly related to the task?

Index

ability   29, 197
abnormal   184, 246
abroad   133
absences   229
absent 229
acceptable   56, 84, 95, 141, 190
acceptance   6, 118, 147, 223, 249, 256
accepted   105, 148, 180, 229
accepting   155
access 2, 9-10, 23, 66, 154, 235
accomplish   7, 82, 103, 124, 191, 232
according   33, 146, 250
account   11, 29, 55, 152, 188, 241
accounting   189, 241
accrue 136
accuracy   147, 192
accurate   10, 107
accurately   233, 254
achievable   117, 191
achieve   7, 69, 74, 83, 112, 114, 158, 186-187, 205, 213,
231, 243
achieved   19, 76, 84, 123, 191, 249
achieves   133
achieving   134, 222
acquire   217
acquired   158, 186
across 47, 182, 218
action 48, 94, 98, 149, 152, 169, 198-199, 215
actionable   44, 118
actions 21, 49, 93, 98, 121, 147, 152, 177, 186, 210, 227, 251
active 154
activities   18, 20, 26, 32, 75, 96, 156-160, 162, 167, 169-170,
176-177, 201, 206, 224
activity 3-4, 39, 135, 148, 156, 158-164, 168, 173, 176, 214, 227,
257
actual 39, 57, 141, 176, 188, 241-242, 247, 257
actually   34, 63, 87, 90, 191, 196, 243
adaptive   233
addition   8, 108
additional   32, 40, 59, 61, 66, 68, 178, 215, 227

additions   97
address   20, 173, 186, 245
addressed   164, 194, 197, 235, 237, 249
addressing   29, 120
adequate   36, 146-147, 174, 215, 231, 254
adequately   32, 228
adherence   139
Adjust 96-97
adjusted   94, 222
adopted   134
adopters   194
advance   230, 253
advantage   69, 102
advantages   109, 257
adverse   152
advertised   253
advice 245
affect 59, 66, 72, 108, 122, 127, 144, 219-221, 231, 259
affected   193, 195, 201, 205, 210, 218
affecting   13, 23, 70
afford 197-198
affordable   86
against32, 91, 93, 146, 153, 168, 225, 231
agencies   202
agendas   110
aggregate   47
agreed   193, 210, 260
agreement   5, 108, 229, 254
agreements   60, 76, 244
agrees 105
aiming 112
alerts   92
aligned   22
alignment   135, 185
aligns   207
alleged   1
allocate   108, 177
allocated   46, 55, 102, 152
allocating   242
allowable   53
allowances   229
allowed   117
allows 10, 172

almost 243
already   124, 183, 217
always 10, 176
Amazon   11
amended   182
amount   21, 148
amplify64, 117
analogous   169
analysis   3, 5, 12, 60, 62-64, 68, 85, 132, 141, 154, 175, 178,
202, 207, 209-210, 218, 220, 232, 241, 245
analytical   245
analyze   2, 58-59, 70, 184, 234
analyzed   44, 92, 141, 147, 193, 245
analyzes   138
annual 180
annually   152
another   11, 150
answer 12-13, 17, 28, 43, 58, 74, 89, 101, 218
answered   27, 41, 57, 73, 88, 100, 125
answering   12, 160, 247
anyone   41, 105, 116
anything   158, 164, 222
appear   1
appetite   200
applicable   13, 90, 139, 142, 152, 222, 245, 247
applied   79, 100, 135, 158, 242
appointed   30, 38
appointing   202
appraise   133
appreciate   191
approach   48, 75, 82, 109, 148, 206, 216, 231-232, 234, 239-
240, 259
approaches   85, 87, 195
approval   32, 120, 141
approvals   193
approve   140, 218
approved   36, 72, 144, 147, 180, 218, 220
approvers   140
approving   144
architect   146
Architects   7
archives   255
arranging   211

articulate   232, 240
ascertain   152
ascribed   200
asking 1, 7
aspect 195
aspects   160
aspiration   232
assess 18, 36, 84, 94, 107, 163, 201
assessed   82, 254
assessing   76, 91
Assessment   4-5, 9-10, 19, 138, 190, 193, 200-201, 207, 231, 233
assets 46, 132, 251
assign 24
assigned   152, 154, 210, 227
assigning   167, 208
Assignment   4, 188
assist   9, 58, 92, 176, 178, 223
assistant   7
associated   142, 202, 209, 225, 234
assume   199
assuming   196, 201
Assumption   3, 148
assurance   21, 139, 192, 215, 223
attached   171
attainable   28, 191
attempted   41
attempting   92
attend 23
attendance   30
attended   30
attending   224
attention   13, 101, 196
attitude   256
attitudes   217
attributes   3, 104, 143, 158, 219
audience   213
audited   192, 256
auditing   26, 93, 104, 189
Auditor 245-246
auditors   245-246
auspices   8
author 1
authority   65, 191, 197, 224, 233, 235, 257

authorized   136, 153, 241, 253, 255-256, 259
automatic   255
available   20, 26, 32, 52, 59, 61, 87, 92, 105, 158, 162, 188, 193, 196, 198, 200, 204, 233, 237, 245, 253
Average   13, 27, 42, 57, 73, 88, 100, 125, 170, 222, 247
avoidance   196
background   11, 161
backing   160
backward   220
balanced   87
bandwidth   247
barriers 116, 236
baseline   4, 111, 132, 146, 180, 206
baselines   35, 38, 180
basics 116
because   201
become   105, 121, 123-124, 144
becomes   197, 222
becoming   115
before 10, 41, 95, 162, 192, 198, 203, 207, 218-219, 231
beginning   2, 16, 27, 42, 57, 73, 88, 100, 125
begins 222
behavior   240, 256
behaviors   18, 48, 223
belief   12, 17, 28, 43, 58, 74, 89, 101, 103
believable   117
believe103, 105, 127
benchmark   184, 233
benefit 1, 18, 21, 48, 97, 169
benefits   18, 47, 50, 61, 67, 101, 104, 116, 119, 122-123, 136, 232-233, 237, 257
better 7, 47, 75, 132, 157, 170, 179, 182, 205, 222, 249, 251
between   65, 144, 148, 155, 189, 194, 215, 236, 246, 257
beyond   240
biggest   76, 176, 192
blinding   63
Blokdyk   8
bother 56
bottleneck   156
bought11
bounce   60, 62
boundaries   37, 230, 245
bounds   37

Breakdown   3, 150, 166
briefed 38
Briefly   169
brings   33
broader   232
broken 70
broker 155
budget   90, 105, 136, 153, 156, 170, 172, 180, 214, 242,
247-248, 250, 252, 259
budgeted   57, 241
budgets   20, 109, 152-153, 252
building   21, 94, 166, 243-244
burden 223
burdensome   246
burn-in 249
business   1, 7, 11, 23, 25, 31, 41, 48, 54, 63, 68, 82, 87, 92,
103, 105, 112, 116-117, 123-124, 139-140, 143, 148, 180, 201, 207,
210, 220, 237, 245-246, 249
button 11
buyers 253
buy-in 115, 249
buyout 136
calculated   168, 241
called 215
candidates   254
cannot 153, 176
capability   18, 193, 260
capable   7, 40
capacities   114, 135
capacity   18, 21, 75, 237, 239
capital 121
capitalize   69
capture   44, 95, 184, 255
captured   46, 70, 86, 119, 138, 154, 192-193, 210
capturing   176
career 144
careers   121
carried 71
caseload   230
catalog   253
category   29
caused   1, 51
causes 46, 50, 53, 58-60, 69, 93, 153, 204

causing   23, 211
celebrate   75, 227
celebrated   231
center 51
centrally   87
certain 192, 210
Certified   154-155, 210
chaired   8
challenge   7, 260
challenges   110, 160, 214
champions   186
chances   200
change   5, 17, 19, 35, 44, 52, 65-66, 68, 70, 76, 79, 82, 87,
96, 115, 130-131, 147, 174-175, 180-181, 198, 203, 207, 212-213,
215, 218-221, 235, 238, 255-256, 260
changed   25, 35, 77, 97, 109, 173, 178, 181, 225
changes   24, 33, 38-39, 47, 72, 95, 97, 109, 118, 120, 136-
138, 143, 152, 172, 180, 189, 193, 203, 210-211, 218-221, 228, 231,
233, 241, 254-255, 258
changing   96
channels   237
chargeable   189
charged   48, 241
charges   176
Charter   2, 28, 81, 129-130
charting   210
charts 64, 173
cheaper   47
checked   70, 93, 95, 98
checklist   8
checklists   9
checks 154
choice 29, 111
choices   169
choose   12, 81
chosen 129, 134-135, 200, 204, 214, 251
circumvent   22
claimed   1
clarify 118
classes 192, 207
clearly 12, 17, 26, 28, 33, 38-39, 43, 58-59, 74, 89, 101, 138-139,
190, 229, 239, 253, 260
client   8, 11, 48, 113, 204, 250-251

clients 25, 29, 237, 246
closed 91, 211, 221, 255
closely 11
Close-Out   6, 255, 257
closest 112
Closing6, 61, 251
coaches   186
cognitive   239
cognizant   231
coherent   211
colleague   109
colleagues   106, 110
collect 68, 178, 187, 227, 231
collected   31, 59-60, 65-67, 71, 147, 245
collection   63, 186-187
combine   87
coming   64, 209
command   98
comments   249
commitment 98, 115, 187, 242
committed   63, 138, 148, 155, 175, 206, 246
committee   154
common   146, 172, 176, 194, 209
community   171, 178-179, 204
companies   1, 8, 169
company   7, 47, 69, 102, 105, 107, 109, 113, 116-117
compare   64, 84, 242, 244
compared   107, 153, 202
comparing   85
comparison   12
compatible   220, 254
compelling   31
competing   55
competitor   132, 241
complains   231
complaint   231
complete   1, 9, 12, 26, 33, 39, 156, 158, 168, 171, 184, 196,
198, 203, 246, 249, 255
completed   13, 32, 36, 156, 162, 207, 227, 255
completely   138, 170
completing   104
completion   31, 39, 146, 153, 163, 180-181, 188, 227, 240-241,
243, 251, 254

complex   7, 173, 243
complexity   21, 48, 55, 64
compliance   47, 50, 56, 64, 76, 149, 182, 233, 245
compliant   208
complied   227
component   185
components   148, 206
compute   13
concept   82
conceptual   215
concern   48, 191, 232
concerns   25-26, 112, 194, 235, 248
concrete   78, 239
concurs   208
condition   93
conditions   98, 109, 132, 137, 227, 254
conduct   154, 208
conducted   138, 193, 209, 220, 259
conference   208-209
confidence   185, 200
confident   162
confirm   13, 254
Conflict   141, 230
conflicts   142, 172, 227, 230
conjure   142
connecting   118
consensus   258
consider   18, 22-23, 159
considered   17, 20, 47, 223
considers   69
consistent   34, 46, 94, 176, 196, 241
consortium   203
constant   242
constantly   195
constitute   232
Constraint   3, 148, 246
consultant   7, 177, 201
consulted   113, 194, 235
consulting   56
consumers   109
Contact   7
contacts   102
contain   22, 60, 91, 234

contained   1
contains   9
content   34, 223
contents   1-2, 9, 235
context   30, 36, 38, 215
continual   11, 91-92
continuity   54
continuous   59, 79
contract   6, 152-153, 162, 176, 189, 217, 227-228, 233, 245, 254-256
contracted   254
contractor   6, 127, 168, 201, 247, 254, 259
contracts   32-33, 60, 211, 215, 248, 255
contribute   132, 257
control 2, 46, 61, 89-90, 92-93, 95-99, 132, 138, 147, 152, 172, 179, 188, 215, 218-219, 223, 241
controlled   72, 235, 253, 258
controls   22, 59, 62, 81, 83, 87, 97-100, 163, 245
convention   123
conversion   148
convey   1
cooperate   178
Copyright   1
corporate   224
correct43, 89, 138, 154
corrected   175
corrective   49, 93, 152, 210
correspond   9, 11
costing52, 176
counting   115, 156
counts 115
course 35, 52, 243
covering   9, 99
covers 192
coworker   113
craziest   115
create 11, 17, 72, 109, 115, 117, 147
created   63-64, 97, 131, 135, 137
creating   7, 135, 211
creative   19
creativity   83
credible   178
crisis   20

criteria 2, 5, 9, 11, 28-29, 33, 69, 82, 84, 91, 104, 116, 126, 144, 146-147, 178, 180, 184, 208-209, 256, 260
CRITERION   2, 17, 28, 43, 58, 74, 89, 101
critical 34-35, 64, 86, 92, 99, 114, 134, 148, 155-156, 160, 200, 214, 222
criticism   63
cross-sell   110
crucial 68, 132, 160
crystal 13
culture 39, 70, 190
current 38, 43-44, 54, 62-63, 65, 71, 77, 86, 90, 102-103, 107, 118, 162, 183, 190, 211-212, 230, 251
currently   33, 113
custom 27
customer   11, 22, 29, 31, 33-34, 83, 93, 99, 102, 109, 122-123, 142-143, 180-181, 183, 185, 200, 203, 212
customers   1, 21, 41, 44, 50, 55-56, 63, 71, 94, 104, 108-110, 113, 118-119, 121, 123-124, 132, 146, 148, 155, 160, 184, 201, 211, 217, 228
cut-backs   192
cut-down   243
cycles 130
damage   1, 197
Dashboard   9
dashboards   97
databases   187
dataset   232
day-to-day   92, 118
deadlines   20, 110, 161
dealing   22
debriefing   208
deceitful   113
decide 78, 182, 191
decided   81, 227
deciding   113, 169
decision   5, 60, 79, 82-84, 86, 198, 209, 222-223, 237
decisions   75, 77-78, 80-81, 83, 95-96, 132, 210, 223, 227-228, 234
dedicated   7
deeper   13, 232
defect 192, 207
define 2, 28, 31, 39, 62, 67, 87, 140, 143, 146, 150, 170, 184, 222, 239

defined   12-13, 17, 19, 22, 28-30, 32-36, 38-41, 43, 58, 72,
74, 89, 101, 138-139, 146, 148, 154, 159, 173, 183, 185, 188, 190,
229, 237, 253, 260
defines 18, 29, 41, 166
defining   7, 111
definite   91, 159
definition   26, 30, 36-37, 40, 138, 181, 214
degree   231-232, 234, 239-240
delaying   48
delays 51, 156, 171
delegated   40
delete 177
deletions   97
deliver 21, 35, 83, 123, 179, 224
delivered   44, 104, 140, 172, 252, 257
delivering   233
delivers   166
delivery   107, 109, 134, 162, 256
demand   122, 132, 245
department   7, 116, 188, 216
depend   216
dependent   107, 132
depends   102
deploy 98, 109
deployed   99
deploying   56
deployment   53, 225
derive 91, 160
Describe   25, 141, 144, 161, 247
described   1, 220
describing   169
deserving   217
design 1, 8, 11, 72, 77, 98, 231, 245
designed   7, 11, 68, 84, 254
designing   7
desired 18, 32, 69, 84, 127, 166, 181, 243
detail   48, 84, 146-147, 151, 159, 171
detailed   60, 64, 138-139, 141, 148, 156, 188, 241
details 49, 212
detect 98
detected   210
detection   246

determine   11-12, 110, 122, 135, 156, 178, 201, 209-210, 229, 233-234
determined   72, 122, 155, 186
detracting   112
develop   43, 74-75, 78, 83, 85, 150, 198, 210
developed   8, 11, 28, 31-32, 48, 81, 139, 152, 186-187, 192, 211-212, 214, 220, 234, 238, 243
developers   200
developing   63, 86, 233
device 225
devices   225
diagram   3, 54, 60, 162-163
diagrams   56, 210
Dictionary   3, 152
differ   173
difference   147, 172, 177, 215, 222
different   7, 29, 34, 41, 58, 60, 122-123, 212, 258
differs 208
difficult 69, 158
dilemma   123
dimensions   17
direct 152, 188-189
direction   35, 47
directions   204
directly 1, 63, 71, 132, 152, 194, 260
Directory   5, 227
Disagree   12, 17, 28, 43, 58, 74, 89, 101
disaster   54, 172
discarded   149
discover   253
discovery   237
discussion   117
displayed   67, 157, 170
disposal   225
disputes   230, 232, 255
disqualify   63
disruptive   68
distribute   227
divide 229
Divided   27, 40-41, 57, 73, 88, 100, 125
division 137
Divisions   189
document   11, 140, 147, 149, 222, 227, 252

documented 40, 84, 90-91, 96, 99, 142, 148-149, 154-155, 168,
180, 183-184, 190-192, 211, 237, 253
documents   7, 153, 168, 234, 254
dollars 188
domains   80
dormant   102
drawing   200
Driver 64
drivers 51, 63
drives 49
driving 108, 121
duplicates   141
Duration   3-4, 134, 168, 170
durations   39
during 35, 80, 149, 164, 174, 189, 208, 212, 225, 254, 259
dynamic   48
dynamics   37
earlier 117
earliest 140
Earned 5, 176, 188, 243
easily   147
economic   202, 204
economical   114, 136
economies   132
Economy   133
eDiscovery   222
edition 9
editorial   1
educate   251
education   23, 96
effect 155, 198, 257
effective   24, 104, 114-115, 148, 152, 224-226, 245
effects 45, 132, 232
efficiency   71, 91, 169
efficient   81, 134-135, 216, 254
effort   38, 50, 53, 102, 140, 148, 153, 206, 235, 238
efforts 41, 79, 207
either   159
electronic   1
element   152, 154
elements   11-12, 41, 65, 94, 122, 147, 153, 189, 211, 227,
231, 241
Elevator   143

elicit   187
eliminate   231
embarking   31
emergent   48
emerging   66, 93, 233
emphasis   222
employed   175
employee   78, 112, 201, 233, 247
employees   18, 23, 25, 68, 106, 116, 233-234, 253-254
employers   131
empower   7
enable 68
enablers   113, 259
encounter   201
encourage   83, 93
end-users   246
engage   108, 230, 236, 239-240
engagement   44, 131, 195
enhance   94
enhanced   121
enhancing   96
enlarged   200
enough   7, 72, 101, 104, 122, 127, 144, 232, 238, 251
ensure 32, 39, 71, 114, 116, 118, 133, 148, 190, 210, 227, 231, 239, 245
ensuring   10, 102, 215, 243
entail   50
entering   245
Enterprise   216
entities 56
entity   1, 142
envisaged   134
equations   168
equipment   20, 201, 229
equitably   40, 229, 239
equivalent   155
errors   117, 176, 245
escalated   177
Escalation   180
essence   129, 231
essential   239
essentials   119
establish   74, 98, 179

estimate   47, 55-56, 169-170, 249
-estimate   181
estimated   31, 39, 47, 112, 179, 199, 247-248
estimates   3-4, 33, 52, 61, 148, 153, 168, 176, 193, 210
estimating   4, 139, 154, 170, 178, 206
estimation   85, 175, 206
estimator   176
etcetera   55, 109
ethical 17, 107, 249
ethnic 116
evaluate   77-78, 80, 174, 188
evaluated   253
evaluating   82
evaluation   69, 85, 94, 208-209, 240, 254
evaluative   215
evaluators   209
events 23, 76, 82, 84, 189, 241
everyday   68
everyone   37, 40, 147, 230
everything   53
evidence   13, 50, 198, 216, 254
evolution   43, 259
evolve 95
exactly184, 191
examined   34, 253
Example   2, 9, 14, 61, 92, 149
examples   7, 9, 11, 215
exceeding   44, 190
excellence   7, 36
excelling   190
excessive   154
Exclusions   174
execute   127, 238, 251
executed   180, 221, 254
Executing   5, 214
execution   98, 149, 227, 253
executive   7, 175
executives   114
exercise   22
existence   204
existing11-12, 92, 114, 129, 137, 140, 214
exists   162
expansion   192

expect 124, 180, 203, 257
expected   18, 39, 82, 103, 116, 135, 181, 224, 253
expend   53
expenses   230
experience   37, 107, 112, 161, 176, 191, 202, 242, 247
experiment   117
expertise   87, 174, 188
experts 35, 202
expiration   162
explained   11
explicitly   115
explore   60, 234
express 132
expressed   127
extent 12, 18, 21, 32, 77, 135, 245, 259
external   41, 45, 106, 194, 202, 224
facilitate   12, 70, 97, 240
facing 22, 123
factors 81, 112, 148, 161, 178
failed   55, 103, 105
failure 54, 112, 149, 185
fairly   40
familiar9
fashion 1
Favorable   242
feasible   56, 69, 121, 179
feature10
features   250
feedback   2, 11, 31, 34, 55
fidelity 245
Filter   184
finalized   14
financial   54, 61, 67, 102, 123, 132, 160, 197-198, 237, 246
fingertips   10
finish   140, 156, 158, 160-161, 163, 243-244
Fiscal   245
fitness   245
flexible 50
focused   45, 48, 50
follow   11, 90, 119-120, 134, 162, 214, 250
followed   38, 206, 218
following   9, 12
follow-up   45, 134-135

for--and   93
forecast   243
forefront   110
foresee   160
forever 109
forget 10
formal 6, 175, 206, 240, 249
formally   40, 193
format 11, 155, 228
formats   154
forming   148
formula   13, 118
Formulate   28
forward   121
forwarded   189
foster   104, 111, 190
framework   98, 114, 135, 186
freaky 104
frequency   33, 93, 104, 186, 259
frequent   206
frequently   45, 212, 232, 234
friend   107, 109, 123
frontiers   82
full-blown   52
full-scale   77
fulltime 175
function   132, 237, 249, 253
functional   136, 152-153, 229, 233
functions   30, 66, 106, 122, 142, 201, 227
funded180
funding   106, 122, 128, 148, 153, 240
further 198
future   7, 50, 80, 96, 117, 134, 137, 202, 259
gained59, 90, 96
gather 12, 29, 31, 35-37, 39, 43, 67, 71-72
gathered   30, 60, 66-68, 71, 141
gathering   30-31, 142-143
general   82, 169, 249
generally   216
generate   59, 68
generated   60, 128
generation   9, 67, 260
geographic   230

Gerardus	8
getting 56, 188, 194, 223, 235
governance	18, 114, 134, 190, 192, 233
Government	153
graphical	173
graphs 9
greater	134
greatest	79, 260
ground 67, 202
grouped	158
groups 122, 138-139, 148, 166, 193, 210, 216
growth 63, 112
guarantee	82
guidance	1
guidelines	223
handle 164, 200, 228-229
handled	141
handling	201
happen	21, 103, 199, 212, 218
happened	218
happening	205
happens	7, 11, 33, 47, 54, 104, 112, 122, 138, 176, 178, 184,
199, 204, 255
hardest	47
hardly	243
hardware	141, 214-215, 245
havent 124
Having 198
heading	192
health	106
hearing	117
helpful 168, 189
helping	7, 135, 146
Herzberg	169
hidden 49
higher	153, 210
highest 23
high-level	36
Highly	66
high-tech	124
hijacking	117
hinder 190
hindrance	225

hiring   97
historical   178
history 167, 181
hitters 64
hitting 244
holders 139
honest 107
horizon 110
humans   7
hypotheses   58
identified   1, 20-21, 24, 29, 59, 61, 64-65, 81, 86, 134, 153-
155, 159, 168, 174-175, 180, 191, 199, 204, 207, 209, 211, 213,
215, 223, 228, 235, 253, 258, 260
identifier   129
identify 12, 18, 25, 61-62, 66, 130, 147, 152-153, 160, 178, 208,
225, 242
ignore 20
ignoring   114
images 142
imbedded   96
impact 4, 37, 50, 52, 54-56, 117, 177, 180-181, 196, 199-200, 202,
220, 233, 235, 237, 260
impacted   49, 127, 211
impacts   54-55, 149, 170, 183, 257
implement   21, 53, 89, 188
implicit 121
importance   210, 232, 239
important   20, 22, 34, 63, 65, 71, 104, 109-110, 116, 120, 129,
132, 134-135, 180, 188, 195, 209, 212, 234, 238
improve   2, 11-12, 62, 74-75, 77-80, 82-83, 87, 127, 149, 166,
207, 238, 251, 259
improved   76, 79, 98, 132, 134, 225, 251
Improving   217, 246
inactive   177
incentives   97, 233-234
include   23, 87, 136, 141, 175, 207-208, 218, 231
included   2, 9, 19, 53, 142, 154, 170, 179, 202, 247, 255
INCLUDES   10
including   18, 37, 54, 56, 71, 94, 130, 148, 153-154, 200, 235
increase   77, 107, 169, 203
increased   116
increasing   118, 222
incurred   55

incurring   241
in-depth   9, 12
indicate   63, 93, 104
indicated   93, 254
indicators   51, 53, 61, 63, 71, 86, 94, 135, 196
indirect   48, 152, 177, 241-242
indirectly   1
individual   1, 44, 156, 175, 182, 191, 257-258
industry   97, 107, 174
influence   82, 119, 131, 135, 191, 222-223, 235
influences   194
inform 231
informal   240
informed   119, 139, 232, 253
ingrained   94
inherent   107, 190
in-house   259
initial   36, 113, 130
initially 33
initiate 152
initiated   178, 221
Initiating   2, 118, 127
Initiation   259
initiative   12, 129, 182, 186-187, 195, 235
Innovate   74
innovation   50, 61, 71, 94, 111, 182
innovative   109, 179
in-process   61
inputs 29, 45, 59, 95
inside   25
insight 61, 68
insights 9
inspired   113
instead 102, 168
integrate   81, 107
integrity   23, 120, 220
intended   1, 74, 198
INTENT 17, 28, 43, 58, 74, 89, 101
intention   1
intentions   132, 225
interact   122
interest 111, 184, 195, 216
interests   21, 257

interface   245
interfaces   148
interim 110
internal   1, 41, 71, 106, 119, 148, 189, 192, 194
interpret   12-13
intervals   175, 192
interview   111, 257
introduce   48
introduced   237
invalid 154
invaluable   2, 11
invariably   253
invest 61
investment   66, 186, 200
invoices   192
involve 112, 215
involved   19, 21, 35, 47, 59, 66, 86, 119, 134, 138-139, 141,
146, 148, 188, 190, 202, 214, 216, 233, 246, 256
involves   91
issues   20, 22, 24-27, 132, 142, 147, 164, 172, 175, 177, 193, 227,
235
itself   1, 26
jointly   231, 239
judgment   1
justified100, 148
killer   109
knowledge   11, 32, 37, 41, 59, 79, 87, 90, 94, 96-98, 102, 104,
107, 182, 191, 255
labeled   188
lacked 97
largely 62
larger   50
largest 169
latest   9, 153
laundry   141
Leader 1-6, 9-15, 17-27, 29-42, 44-92, 94-107, 109-142, 144, 146-
150, 152, 154-160, 162-164, 166, 168-176, 178-180, 182-184, 186,
188, 190-198, 200-204, 206-208, 210-212, 214-222, 224, 227, 229,
231, 233, 235, 237-241, 243-247, 249-253, 255, 257-260
leaders37, 62-63, 98, 103, 105, 109, 115, 120-121, 138, 155, 194,
206
leadership   22, 40, 106, 109, 147
learned   6, 95, 119, 186, 249, 257-259

learning   94, 97, 226
length 229
lesson 257
lessons 6, 77, 95, 119, 186, 249, 258-259
Leveling   159
levels   18, 23, 32, 63, 71, 86, 96-97, 106, 150, 153, 183, 187
leverage   40, 95, 112, 178
leveraged   41
leveraging   233
levers 213
liability 1
licensed   1
lifecycle   52, 62
lifecycles   87
Lifetime   10
likelihood   74, 77, 134, 205
likely   80, 90, 109, 208
limitation   48
limited 11, 153, 191
linked 29, 142, 222
listed   1, 188
listen   110, 118, 229
little   141
locally 88
logical 162, 164, 241
longer 98
long-term   97, 102, 104
Looking   24
losing 56
losses 25, 34
lowest 241
magnitude   79
maintain   89, 112, 120, 127, 180
maintained   80, 153, 225, 240
makers 84, 90, 237
making   24, 60, 79, 82, 115, 186-187, 192, 198, 260
manage   30, 38, 41, 43, 45, 52, 62, 75-76, 83, 87, 102, 124,
136, 144, 149, 164, 172, 174, 182, 187, 189, 195, 202, 235
manageable 34, 81, 206
managed   7, 35, 65, 69, 74, 77, 82, 84-85, 91, 96, 140, 146,
169, 249

management 1, 3-5, 9, 11-12, 21-22, 55, 58-59, 64-66, 70, 77, 79, 81, 83, 86-87, 102, 112, 115-116, 119, 132, 134-140, 146-147, 152-155, 159, 166-167, 169-170, 174-176, 182-183, 187-188, 191-194, 196-198, 206-207, 209-212, 214, 216, 218, 223, 225, 227, 237-238, 243, 245, 249, 251, 255
manager 7, 12, 26, 32, 39, 154, 202, 207, 210, 216, 249
managers 2, 126, 152, 189, 200, 215
manages 75, 86, 137, 248
managing 2, 84, 126, 131, 203, 211, 225, 235
mandatory 220, 258
manner 25, 83, 148, 152, 218, 241, 249
mantle 112
Mapping 74
market 130, 132, 197, 241, 243
marketable 197
marketer 7
marketing 109, 226
markets 20
Maslow 169
material 129, 184, 242, 254
materials 1, 210, 230
matrices 144
Matrix 3-4, 132, 144-145, 185, 188, 202
matter 35, 51, 53, 231
matters 222
maximize 200, 233
maximizing 101
McClellan 169
McGregor 169
meaningful 56, 118, 234
measurable 28, 33, 128, 225, 239, 253
measure 2, 12, 24, 26, 33, 40, 43-46, 49, 52, 55, 64, 71, 74, 77-79, 85, 91-92, 99, 134-135, 146, 178, 184-186, 231
measured 22, 43-45, 47, 50, 53-54, 56, 84, 91, 95, 239
measures 45, 47, 51-52, 54-55, 61, 63, 71, 86, 93-94, 97, 134, 183-184, 205, 219, 233-234, 246
measuring 96
mechanical 1
mechanism 203
mechanisms 134-135
mechanized 174
mediated 230
medium 231, 243

meeting   32, 38, 93, 148, 180, 195, 217, 227, 229, 257
meetings   29-30, 36, 189, 192, 223, 229, 237
megatrends   116
member   5, 40, 106, 123, 166, 216, 233, 235
members   40, 62, 92, 139, 175, 189, 191, 206, 228-232, 234, 239-240
membership   231, 240
memorable   234
message   91, 212-213
messages   194
method   49, 176, 194, 219, 231-232
methods   33-34, 56, 72, 175, 178, 212, 245
metrics 4, 40, 58, 97, 140-141, 174, 176, 184, 193, 212
milestone   3, 154, 160-162, 168
milestones   131, 158, 162
minimize   172, 196
minimizing   62, 101
minimum   225, 247
minority   21
minutes   38, 86, 227
missed 52, 117
missing 66, 118, 158
mission 69, 72, 106, 120, 205, 253
mistakes   260
mitigate   86, 147
mitigated   258
mitigating   155
mitigation   211
mix-ups   225
modeling   62
models53, 61, 102
modern   206
modified   98, 218
module   140
moment   120
moments   68
momentum   101, 117
monetary   21
monitor   92, 95-96, 178, 238
monitored   91-92, 95, 155-156, 168, 170, 253
monitoring   5, 92, 94, 96, 99-100, 140, 164, 196, 210, 219, 237, 253
monthly   242

months 76, 86
motivate 111, 240
motivated 127
motivation 26, 93
multiple 140, 175
mutual 135
narrative 160
narrow 68
national 204, 214
nature 48, 152
nearest 13
nearly 105
necessary 61, 67, 70, 102, 109, 120, 178, 197, 212, 220, 224, 228, 237
needed 18-19, 21, 24-27, 29, 59, 67, 72, 92, 94-95, 99, 135, 143, 178, 186, 192, 212, 214-215, 237, 260
negative 106, 213
negotiate 113
negotiated 108, 212
neither 1
network 3, 162-163, 235
networks 214
Neutral 12, 17, 28, 43, 58, 74, 89, 101
nominated 213
normal 94
notice 1, 169
noticing 222
notified 196, 255
notify 229
noting 218
number 27, 41, 57, 73, 88, 100, 125, 158, 166, 246, 261
numbers 108, 169, 230
numerous 255
objection 25
objective 7, 56, 129-130, 139, 147, 200, 222
objectives 19, 22, 28-29, 36, 69, 72, 91, 104, 109, 115, 123, 168, 174, 180, 194, 198, 205, 207, 217, 233, 239
observing 149
obsolete 116
obstacles 22, 179
obtain 118, 249, 253, 257
obtained 31, 127, 141
obtaining 45

obviously   13
occurrence   196
occurring   200
occurs 20, 95, 127, 185, 237
offerings   64, 84
office   208, 216, 255
officials255
offshore   142
offsite   202
onboarding   174
one-time   7
ongoing   83, 95, 156, 170
online   11
on-site   227
operate   180, 204, 230
operates   107
operating   5, 52, 54, 94, 135, 188, 229
operation   90
operations   12, 94, 96-97
operators   90
opinion   210
opponents   194
opposite   103, 107
opposition   118
optimal   83, 247
optimize   82, 96
optimized   122
option 111
options26, 198
organized   158
orient 93
original172, 207, 222
originate   90
others 141, 174, 178, 180, 194, 197, 203, 235, 239, 251
otherwise   1
outcome   13, 82, 128, 141, 166, 253
outcomes   87, 96, 112, 133, 135, 179, 198, 226, 243, 245, 257
outlier 159
outlined   91
output 40, 59-61, 64-65, 67, 69, 72, 93, 98, 146
outputs   58-59, 61, 72, 95, 135, 164, 225
outside83, 130, 214-215, 232, 237
Outsource   71, 255

outsourced   215
overall 12-13, 22, 46, 103, 106, 134, 163, 223, 229, 237-238, 248
overcome   179
overhead   152, 189, 242
overheads   139
overlook   194, 236
overlooked   127
overruns   242
overseas   201
oversight   65, 155, 233
overtime   164
ownership   38, 98, 135
package   188, 241
packages   188
Padding   177
paradigms   118
paragraph   106
parameters   92
paramount   196
Pareto 64, 210
particular   61, 200, 224, 232, 254
Parties 136, 224, 256
partners   21, 35, 94, 101, 109, 135, 201, 237
patterns   75
paycheck   116
paying 101
payment   132, 192-193, 206, 256
payments   253
pending   221
people7, 24, 50, 58, 63, 85-86, 93, 96, 102, 104-105, 108-110, 112,
114, 121-122, 127, 132, 154, 186, 188, 196, 198, 200, 205, 211-212,
214, 217, 232, 238, 243, 245, 251
perceive   115
perceived   232
percent   117
percentage   144, 184
perception   79-80, 107
perform   24, 29, 40, 141, 148, 154, 156, 218, 249
performed   83, 144, 157, 168, 174, 188, 196, 241
perhaps   25, 243
period 84
permission   1
permit 48

person 1, 24, 132
personal 119, 259
personally 144
personnel 21, 23, 70, 92, 174, 186-187, 200, 259
pertinent 92
phases 52, 86, 158, 194
pitfalls 107
placements 225
planet 96
planned 91, 97, 100, 133, 141, 153, 158, 170, 229, 241, 260
planners 90
planning 3, 9, 92, 95, 134, 146, 148, 152, 162, 164, 182, 216, 224, 259
platforms 233
players 80
pocket 171
pockets 171
points 27, 41, 57, 60, 73, 88, 100, 124, 161, 186-187
policies 190
policing 245
policy 36, 75, 90, 135, 149, 164, 192, 198, 224, 254
political 30, 105, 134
portfolio 105, 238
portfolios 195, 235
portray 64
position 190
positioned 178
positive 76, 106, 117
possess 231
possible 55-56, 59, 68, 82, 89, 111, 146, 170, 192, 207, 224, 253
potential 17, 63, 77, 81, 105, 116, 146, 199, 204, 236-237, 242
practical 69, 74, 86, 89, 217
practice 253
practices 1, 11, 62, 75, 95, 97, 190, 206, 215, 233, 250
precaution 1
precede 162
predicting 96
predictor 166
pre-filled 9
prepare 229
prepared 174

preparing   231, 258
present   96, 111, 117, 201, 213
presented   26, 218, 228
preserve   30
preserved   61
pressures   161
prevent   51
prevented   225
preventive   205
prevents   24
previous   41, 160, 247
previously   136, 220
prices   242, 253
primary   46
principles   135, 206
printing   8
priorities   44, 47-48, 55
prioritize   182
priority 56, 159, 232
privacy   38, 137
private 253
probable   202
probably   166
problem   17, 19, 21, 23-26, 28, 32, 41, 44, 56, 59, 69, 142, 210, 217, 222, 243
problems   19, 22-24, 26-27, 83, 85, 93, 114, 134, 147, 184, 186, 209, 238
procedure   225
procedures   11, 84, 90-91, 94, 96, 139, 149, 155, 164, 169, 173, 175, 182-184, 218, 223, 245
proceed   196, 201, 241
process   1-7, 11, 29, 31, 34, 36, 38, 40, 44, 58-60, 62-68, 70-72, 89-90, 92-94, 96, 98, 127, 134, 139-140, 143-144, 146, 148-149, 154, 164, 172, 174, 176, 182, 186-187, 190, 196, 200, 206-208, 211, 214, 223, 227-228, 237, 243, 245, 248-249, 251
processes   46, 54, 58, 61-62, 64-66, 68-72, 92, 94, 97, 134-135, 138-139, 148, 174, 210-211, 214, 220, 224-225, 237, 250-251, 254
produce   65, 135, 164, 176, 217, 227
produced   64, 76, 237
producing   144, 146
product   1, 11, 47, 63, 71, 103, 109, 180, 183, 197, 200, 216-217, 220, 235, 243-244, 246, 251-252, 257
production   35, 83, 116, 132

products 1, 20, 108, 129-130, 134, 144, 155, 181, 210, 217, 245, 260
program 20, 48, 64, 130, 134-135, 177, 197, 214, 235, 237
programme 237
programs 195, 217-218, 235
progress 38, 43, 78, 115-116, 134, 146, 178, 186-187, 206, 225, 231, 238
project2-7, 9, 23-25, 27, 32, 52, 62, 66, 83, 91, 97, 105-107, 112, 116, 119, 126-142, 144, 146-148, 150, 152, 154-160, 162-163, 166, 168-176, 178-180, 183-184, 188, 190-198, 200-203, 206-207, 210-211, 214-221, 235, 237-240, 243, 246-247, 249-252, 255, 257-260
projected 180
projects 2, 55, 110, 117, 126, 134-135, 144, 146-147, 149-150, 169, 172, 180, 182, 195, 202, 215-217, 227, 235, 243-244, 257, 260
promising 109
promote 63, 182
promptly 177, 231
proper 193
properly 11, 37, 40, 201, 203, 219, 253
proponents 194
proportion 259
Proposal 160, 252
proposals 90, 209
proposed 21, 47, 55, 136, 175, 247, 252
protect 62, 124, 137
protected 61, 229
protection 101
proved250
proven210
provide 20, 61, 114, 120, 124, 131, 139, 152, 162, 168-169, 176, 179, 184, 189, 240
provided 8, 13, 90, 168, 174, 208, 212, 229, 246
provider 213
providing 131, 147, 160, 173, 181, 224
provision 206, 223
public 226, 253
publisher 1
pulled 117
purchase 9, 11, 208-209, 254
purchased 11
purchases 253
purchasing 254

purpose 2, 11, 106, 129-130, 167, 178, 181, 210, 219, 231-232, 234, 239, 260
pushing 105
qualified 40, 62, 65-66, 154
qualifies 66, 72
qualify 55, 66, 69
qualities 24
quality 1, 4-5, 11, 21, 49, 51, 59-60, 70, 81, 95, 97, 118, 134-135, 139, 155, 182-185, 187, 190-192, 201, 210, 215, 223-224, 245, 254
quantified 96
quantify 55
quantity 254
question 12-13, 17, 28, 43, 58, 74, 89, 101, 113, 187, 230, 235
questions 7, 9, 12, 69, 141, 168, 170, 197, 209, 215
quickly 12, 60-62
quotations 253
radically 68
raised 147
raters 234
rather 48, 119
rating 208
ratings 208-209
rationale 222
reached 25
reaching 115
reactivate 102
readiness 35, 138
readings 95
realism 209
realistic 25, 71, 112, 127, 136, 172, 232
reality 154, 197
realize 48, 234
realized 116, 249
really 7, 21, 39, 140
reason 103, 119
reasonable 80, 122, 136-137, 176, 192, 210
reasons 31, 152
reassess 206
reassigned 180
rebuild 109
receipt 225
receive 9-10, 39, 47, 132, 208

received   38, 119, 197
receives   233
recently   11
recipient   18, 255
recognised   80
recognize   2, 17, 20-22, 24-25, 50, 75, 77
recognized   17-19, 21, 23, 25, 27, 72, 174
recognizes   26
recommend   109, 123, 232
recorded   182
recording   1, 218, 229, 253
records   59, 153, 189, 225, 255
recovery   54, 149
recruiting   224
recurrence   204
redefine   25, 29
re-design   70
reduce 45, 50, 152, 223, 231
reducing   93, 118
references   261
reflect 59, 98-99, 258
reflected   240
reform 52, 90, 119, 121
reforms 21, 55-56
refuses 204
regarding   113, 119, 211, 217
Register   2, 4, 131, 141, 198
regret 79
regular 29, 38, 72, 247, 253
regularly   30, 180, 237
regulation   203, 234
regulatory   201, 227, 260
reimbursed   230
reinforced   135
relate   69, 169, 220
related 56, 71, 97, 141, 147, 183, 194-195, 219, 235, 243, 260
relation   18, 20, 82, 106, 226
relations   106, 226
relative 209, 232, 239
release 194
releases   247
relevant   11, 28, 56, 61, 98, 120, 135, 190, 227
reliable 204

relocation   136
remain 242
remaining   178
remotely   189
remunerate   78
repair 192, 207
repeat 212
repeatable   196
rephrased   11
replace   45, 251
replacing   140
replicated   257
report 5-6, 77, 95, 138, 206, 208, 216, 239, 247, 258, 260
reported   153, 208, 210, 236, 243
reporting   64, 99, 106, 140, 153-154, 218, 241
reports 47, 99, 131, 140, 182, 189
represent   84, 181, 220, 252
reproduced   1
reputation   123
request   5, 69, 175, 180-181, 207, 218, 220-221
requested   1, 209, 219-220
requests   203, 208, 218-219
require 32, 52, 60, 92, 98, 129, 164, 173, 234
required   24, 32, 35, 37, 39-40, 45, 49, 60, 70, 78-80, 97, 127,
133, 142, 156, 158-159, 162, 168, 171, 187, 191, 198, 225, 245,
254, 258-259
requiring   131, 255
research   109, 113, 161, 225
reserved   1
reserves   153
reside 78, 177
resistance   213
resolution   61, 84, 230
resolve 22, 24, 227, 232
resolved   177, 230
Resource   3-4, 110, 148, 164, 166, 192, 211, 216
resources   2, 9, 18-20, 23, 32, 36, 45, 69, 79, 97, 99, 102, 108,
110, 127, 132-133, 141, 146, 158, 162, 166, 168, 174, 178, 180,
210, 214, 224, 229, 237, 246, 258
respect   1
respond   134, 199, 213
responded   13
responding   199

response   20, 91, 93, 96, 99, 213, 247, 259
responses   87, 106, 198, 208
responsive   171, 179
result   61, 76, 84, 178, 184, 195, 213, 220, 225, 239, 255, 257-258
resulted   100
resulting   67
results   9, 35, 39, 50, 63, 74-75, 77-78, 82, 84, 87, 90, 94, 127, 134-
135, 138, 158, 178, 182, 187
Retain 101
retention   45
retrospect   117
return   76, 102, 186, 200
returns 202
revenue   26, 47
revenues   46
review 11-12, 35, 45, 59, 162, 176, 181, 189, 211, 222, 224-225,
234, 259
reviewed   31, 168, 175
reviewer   231
reviews 11, 162, 193, 209
revised 61, 100, 153
revisions   255
revisit 222
reward 44, 59, 217
rewarded   23
rewards   97
rework 49, 53
rights   1
rotated   253
routine 91
rushing 195
safely 245
safety 136, 246
sample 168, 208
sampling   210
satisfied   118, 227, 251, 259
satisfies 243
satisfying   108
savings 33, 47-48, 61
scalable   85
scenario   34, 41
schedule   3-4, 33, 51, 90, 107, 153-155, 162, 168-169, 172-
175, 180, 199, 207, 210, 218, 220, 227-228, 247

scheduled   140, 174, 192, 207, 237, 241, 254
schedules   154, 169, 172, 174, 188, 241
scheduling   139, 154, 174
scheme   91
science   62
scopes 147
Scorecard   2, 13-15
scorecards   97
Scores 15
scoring 11
screening   245
second   13
section 13, 27, 41-42, 57, 73, 88, 100, 124-125
sector 243
securing   44, 102
security   26, 60, 78, 94, 131, 148-149, 220
segments   41, 122
select 70
selected   82, 137, 178, 202
selecting   116
selection   5, 208-209, 233
sellers 1
selling 123, 161
senior 98, 106, 109, 116
sensitive   30, 46, 134
sequence   156, 162
sequencing   121, 135, 138
series 12
service 1-2, 7-8, 11, 47, 79-80, 97, 109, 180, 183, 197-198, 208,
216-217
services   1, 8, 32, 56, 105, 108, 114, 169, 210, 215, 224, 247,
249, 255
session 152
setbacks   60, 62
setting 112, 114
several 8, 58, 202
severance   225
severely   70
severity   199
shared 90, 142, 178, 223
sharing 79, 94, 127, 182, 212
shifted 201
shifts 19

shortly 254
short-term   200, 232
should 7, 17, 20, 22-23, 30, 34, 39, 47, 55-56, 59, 61-62, 69-70, 79,
81-82, 91, 97, 110, 114, 117, 121-122, 131, 135, 139-141, 146, 148,
156, 159, 166, 170, 176, 182, 184, 190, 196-198, 200, 202-204, 209,
212, 215, 220, 228, 234, 238, 245, 258
signatures   164
signers 255
signing 182
similar 32, 41, 64, 84, 158, 167, 181, 194
simple 239, 243, 254
simply 9, 11, 223
single   106, 152, 176, 260
single-use   7
situation   19, 43, 173, 237, 243
situations   96
skeptical   109
skills   18, 20, 69, 104, 110, 127, 161, 168, 176, 191, 193, 196,
198, 245, 260
smaller 135
smallest   19, 76
social   109, 133, 204, 254
software   140-141, 172, 176, 193, 200, 206, 214-215, 245,
247
solicit   34
solution   57, 61, 69, 74-77, 81, 84-86, 89, 146, 204, 247
solutions   52, 77, 80-81, 85, 87
solved 17
Someone   7
something   105, 139
Sometimes   52
source 5, 106, 119, 148, 177, 204, 208-209
sources   29, 60, 64
special 32, 90
specific   9, 26, 28, 33, 36, 66, 119, 149, 158, 160, 164, 191,
216, 220, 231, 251
specified   115, 153, 241, 252, 257
Speech   143
sponsor   22, 136, 174, 212
sponsors   21, 187, 228, 237
spread 89, 91
stable 202
staffed 32

staffing 18, 97, 148
stages 206, 225
standard 7, 95, 97, 165, 241, 247
standards 1, 11-12, 89-90, 94, 96, 139, 155, 183-184, 210, 220, 242, 253
started 9
starting 12
startup 129
start-up 227
stated 115-116, 183
statement 3, 12, 83, 85, 129, 146-147, 149
statements 13, 27-28, 41, 57, 59, 73, 88, 100, 125, 147, 187
statistics 147
status 5-6, 63, 152, 175, 192, 206, 216, 241, 243, 247
statute 201, 234
statutory 227
steady 51
steering 154, 175
storage 240
stories 37
strategic 44, 80, 109, 115, 129, 207, 246
strategies 87, 94, 118-119, 211-212, 222-223
strategy 22, 38, 46, 78, 81, 94, 103, 108, 124, 148, 194, 196, 198, 211, 223
Stream 74
strengths 161, 208, 250
stretch 114
strict 70
strive 114
strong 191
Strongly 12, 17, 28, 43, 58, 74, 89, 101
structural 231
structure 3, 49, 83, 114, 146, 150-151, 153, 166, 201, 212, 225
structured 111, 206
structures 189, 240
stubborn 113
stupid 103
subdivide 153
subdivided 188
subject 9-10, 35
Subjective 185
subjects 66

submit 11
submitted 11, 220
subset 19
succeed 50, 102, 161
success 23-24, 31, 33, 35, 37, 40, 45, 49, 54, 77, 80, 83, 85, 91, 102, 104, 109-110, 112, 117-118, 134, 147, 176, 184, 192, 212, 216, 222, 238-239, 257, 260
successes 122
successful 63, 87, 90, 107, 119, 121, 166, 180, 196, 215, 217
succession 93
suddenly 201
sufficient 201, 233, 237
suggest 196, 218, 235
suggested 93, 181, 220
suitable 227
summarize 169
summarized 153
summary 189
supervisor 191, 233
supplied 254
supplier 86, 122, 201
suppliers 71-72, 109, 253-254
supplies 155, 250
supply 51, 254
support 7, 23, 60, 90, 94, 97, 114, 116, 118, 127, 129, 164, 174, 188, 241, 247
supported 60, 214
supporting 78, 175, 186
supportive 190, 206
surface 93
SUSTAIN 2, 82, 101
sustained 238
sustaining 97
symptom 17, 45
system 11-12, 31, 69, 94, 109, 112, 140-142, 152-153, 166, 189, 191, 193, 219-220, 224-225, 241, 243, 246
systematic 48-49
systems 48, 59, 69-71, 77, 83, 97, 147, 149, 182, 214, 224, 226, 241, 243, 245, 250, 253
tackle 45
tactics 222-223
taking 47, 168, 216
talent 65, 106, 192

talents 104, 192
talking 7
target 35, 111, 213
targets 114, 128, 244
tasked 98
teaching   224
teaming   229
technical   87, 132, 148, 160, 168, 200, 208-209
techniques   61, 102
technology   45, 82, 97, 109, 134, 142-143, 169, 202, 230
templates   7, 9
tender 254
testable   34
tested 18
testing 245
Thamhain   169
thankful   8
themes234
themselves   48, 105, 121
theories   169
theory 93
therefore   205
theyre 141
things   76, 110, 127, 196, 207, 215, 238
thinking   62, 83
thorough   85, 220
thoroughly   147
thought   194, 230
threat 25, 120, 231
threats 204
through   70, 72, 109, 153
throughout   1, 62, 117, 162, 168, 242
tighter 109
time-bound   28
timeframe   67, 159, 178
timeframes   24
timeline   185, 220
timely   25, 83, 218, 227, 241, 260
Timescales   161
timetable   163
together   109
tolerances   81
tolerated   170

tomorrow   96, 116
top-down   98
topics 87, 192
toward93, 216
towards   61, 132, 192, 254
traced 181
tracked   155
tracking   41, 140, 148, 174
traction   109
trademark   1
trademarks   1
trade-offs   155
trained37, 182-183, 200
training   20-21, 24-25, 64, 70, 78, 90, 96-97, 168, 197, 212-213, 216, 229, 233
trainings   26
Transfer   13, 27, 42, 57, 73, 88, 97-98, 100, 125, 248
transition   111, 196
translated   33
travel 229
trends 63, 66, 71, 86, 115, 147, 182-183, 204
trigger 81
triggers86, 181, 192
trophy 112
trouble 109
trying 7, 105, 117, 205, 213
turnaround   159
typical 235
ultimate   121
unclear   30
uncovered   143
underlying   85
undermine   105
underruns   242
understand   58, 128, 141, 200, 215, 245
understood   77, 80, 119, 239
undertake   69, 197-198
uninformed   119
unique 123, 161
uniquely   235
universe   246
Unless 7
unpriced   153

unproven   245
unresolved   141, 154, 164
updated   9-10, 59, 163, 206, 219, 252
updates   10, 97, 247
updating   206
upfront212
upload230
up-sell 110
urgent 218
usability   85, 121
useful   80, 95, 150, 197
usefully 12, 20
utility   170
utilized 153, 245
vacations   254
validate   53, 243
validated   31, 36, 60, 72
Validation   243
valuable   7
values 98, 109, 190, 204
variables   59, 98, 222
variance   5, 152, 169, 231-232, 241-242
-variance   180
variances   152-153, 175, 210, 241
variation   17, 39, 60, 64, 93
variations   143
variety 85
various 132, 206
vendor76, 127, 162, 192, 211, 245
vendors   20, 174, 253
verified10, 31, 36, 60, 161
verify   43, 45, 47, 49-51, 53-54, 56, 91, 96, 99, 134, 147, 180, 241, 244, 256
verifying   44, 47, 50, 54
version 247, 261
versions   29, 34
versus   141
vested 111
viable 80, 151
vice-versa   257
viewpoint   258
viewpoints   258
vigorously   239

violate 149
Virtual 229
vision   109
visual   184
visualize   157, 170
voices 131
volatility   246
volume   242
Volumes   132
warrant   227
warranty   1
weaknesses   138, 208, 250
whether   7, 91, 113, 130, 191, 233, 253-254
-which 202
widespread   93
Wilemon   169
windfall   136
window   159
within 69, 84, 146, 153, 156, 170, 185, 191, 204, 217, 220, 225, 230, 250
without1, 13, 109, 112, 196, 201, 220, 255
workdays   199
worked   136, 194
workers   117
workforce   18, 86, 108-109, 122
working   91, 97, 149, 191, 202
Worksheet   4, 170, 178
worried   231
worst-case   34
writing 11, 144
written 1, 224-225
yesterday   22
youhave   152, 172
yourself   112, 117, 123

CPSIA information can be obtained
at www.ICGtesting.com
Printed in the USA
BVHW071117180719
553828BV00015B/1692/P